THE INFLUENCE
OF SEA POWER ON ANCIENT HISTORY

THE INFLUENCE
OF SEA POWER
ON ANCIENT HISTORY

Chester G. Starr

New York   Oxford
OXFORD UNIVERSITY PRESS
1989

Oxford University Press

Oxford   New York   Toronto
Delhi   Bombay   Calcutta   Madras   Karachi
Petaling Jaya   Singapore   Hong Kong   Tokyo
Nairobi   Dar es Salaam   Cape Town
Melbourne   Auckland

and associated companies in
Berlin   Ibadan

Library of Congress Cataloging-in-Publication Data
Starr, Chester G., 1914–
The influence of seapower on ancient history / Chester G. Starr.
    p. cm. Bibliography: p. 101. Includes index.
ISBN 0-19-505666-3   ISBN 0-19-505667-1 (pbk.)
1. Mediterranean Region—History, Naval. I. Title.
DE61.N3S73 1988   909′.09822—dc 19   88-11753

Printing (last digit): 9 8 7 6 5 4 3 2 1

Printed in the United States of America
on acid-free paper

To
Adrienne, Art, Dick, Joan,
John, Josh, and Tom
in deep thanks

Preface

Once again I am grateful for the encouragement of Nancy Lane at Oxford University Press, who has provided wise counsel as in several earlier books; she has become a valued friend as well as a sagacious editor.

To explain the list of names in my dedication: Arther Ferrill and Thomas Kelly assembled and edited my essays for publication by Brill; John and Joan Eadie, with Josiah Ober and Adrienne Mayor, produced a magnificent Festschrift; Richard Mitchell had much to do with my honorary degree from Illinois. Three have been my students, two have been warm-hearted colleagues for a number of years. I am much indebted to them.

Ann Arbor, Michigan   Chester G. Starr
March 1988

Contents

Maps

THE INFLUENCE
OF SEA POWER ON ANCIENT HISTORY

Introduction

Early in the 1880's a captain in the United States navy, stationed off Peru, received an invitation to lecture on naval history at the new Naval War College, soon to open its doors. Alfred Thayer Mahan already had a scholarly reputation; he could not have guessed that this opportunity would lead him to become the most influential theorist of sea power in modern times.

First he had to choose a topic and do some reading. The latter was not an easy task, but fortunately the English Club of Callao extended its hospitality to American officers. In its library Mahan came upon Mommsen's *History of Rome*. As he commented in his autobiography, "It suddenly struck me, whether by some chance phrase of the author I do not know, how different things might have been could Hannibal have invaded Italy by sea."[1] By the time he returned to the United States in 1885 the framework of *The Influence of Sea Power upon History 1660–1783* was firmly set.

Actually Mommsen, while stressing that Rome was mistress of the western Mediterranean at the beginning of the Second Punic War, had not flatly said that Hannibal could not have gone to Italy by sea, but that he chose the land route for reasons which were not entirely obvious; probably, suggested Mommsen, he preferred not to expose his forces "to the unknown and less calculable contingencies of a sea voyage and of naval war."[2] As we shall see in a later chapter, the real explanation was of a different order, not directly connected to sea power; but no matter, Mahan's emphasis on the importance of naval superiority fitted magnificently into the bellicose, imperialistic outburst of the late nineteenth century in the United States, Great Britain, and Germany. He was awarded honorary degrees by both Oxford and Cambridge, and Kaiser Wilhelm II enthusiastically telegraphed that his naval officers were "devouring Captain Mahan's book." It would have been an indigestible diet, for Mahan's prose was lackluster and his theoretical analyses superficial, yet his work has been listed as one of the most influential books ever written.[3]

In view of the enduring popularity of Mahan's comments among modern historians it is not surprising that students of ancient history have likewise tended to emphasize the role of sea power in classical times: "In the Mediterranean world the influence of sea power was rarely dormant and sometimes decisive."[4] Even a cursory glance at a map suggests that the Mediterranean Sea was the geographical focus of Greek and Roman civilization and political activity. From Hecataeus in the sixth century onwards descriptions of the peoples on its shore commonly followed the coast line. More generally, the geographer Strabo in the age of Augustus asserted, "In a sense we are amphibious, and belong no more to the land than to the sea," and in his treatment of Greece followed the practice of the historian Ephorus in using the sea as the base for topographical discussion.[5] Both of the first ancient historians, Herodotus and Thucydides, automatically took the seas as the backdrop for their narratives.

Yet a careful consideration of the fundamental characteristics of ancient political, social, and economic organization might suggest the desirability of a more circumspect assessment of the place of sea power. First, ancient life always and everywhere was rooted in agriculture, for rural productivity was, except in Egypt and a few other favored areas, too limited to support the overwhelmingly urban tilt we now consider normal. So the Roman envoy Censorinus, advising the Carthaginians in 149 B.C., could support his demand that Carthage abandon its seacoast harbors and move 10 miles inland by pointing out how much more stable its position would be.[6] As recently observed, local leaders at Alexandria and other major cities, including even Carthage, were "more likely to derive their wealth from the ownership of land than from active participation in manufacture or even commerce."[7] Political power everywhere naturally resided in the hands of agriculturally rooted elements.

Secondly, maritime commerce itself was throughout antiquity not "the base of power and prosperity,"[8] but rather was largely devoted to the transport of luxury items for these aristocrats: cargoes of "ivory and apes and peacocks, sandal-wood, cedarwood and sweet white wine."[9] Consequently it was less likely to be a major concern of political and military policies. Here, to be sure, one must be discriminating in judgment. Metals, including tin, copper, and iron, as well as good stone, were not to be found everywhere; wool and timber often had to be imported as raw materials for local manufactures. From time to time urban agglomerations arose that were large enough to require seaborne grain, such as Athens in the fifth and fourth centuries B.C. and the city of Rome from at least the third century on down to the end of antiquity. In both examples control of the seas was to be a conscious concern, but by and large most communities were small enough to be fed from their countryside.

And finally the deliberate exercise of sea power depended upon the rise of firm political units with sufficient resources to support navies. Armies can often live off the land and in antiquity did not need continuous supplies of ammunition and other necessities; ships on the other hand have always been expensive, and their crews usually have to be paid. Throughout the prehistoric stage, which lasted in most parts of the Mediterranean to almost 500 B.C., political structures were too amorphous even to dream of naval command or see its utility; only in Egypt and Syria do we find exceptions.

Thalassocracy, thus, requires political and economic systems that can consciously aim at naval control of sea lanes for the transport of useful supplies and also of armies toward that end. Sea power must be able to facilitate and protect a state's commerce and deny that of opposing states, though in classical times the limited seakeeping qualities of galleys severely restricted this role.[10] Instead of viewing sea power as an important element in the course of ancient history, we must expect it to be a spasmodic factor, though at points it does indeed become a critical force.

The point of view encapsulated in Mahan's works must not mislead us. At the outset, let me make it clear that I do not propose to write a general descriptive treatment of ancient seafaring and commerce, or to stray far into technological aspects of the construction of ancient ships; both have been well treated in several recent works.[11] The important matter is the degree to which ships could be and were utilized to support sea power; my approach will be analytical rather than narrative.[12]

CHAPTER I

Ships and Seas

The Mediterranean Sea, to repeat an earlier observation, was the center of Greek and Roman life. Its European shores were sufficiently separated on the north from the rest of the continental landmass by mountain chains to discourage casual interchanges; much of its African coast was guarded by the Saharan desert and the swamps of the upper Nile. At its western end the inland sea, *mare nostrum,* opened into the Atlantic through the strait of Gibraltar; the underwater sill here, known to ancient geographers, led to a difference in water level between the ocean and the Mediterranean that produced a major eastward current in the latter.[1]

To the east lay the Black Sea, approached likewise by the narrow passage of the Hellespont; a downstream current of some six knots required careful navigation by ships bound for the grain, metal, and other products of south Russia and Armenia.[2] Southeast was the Red Sea, connected to the Mediterranean by a canal in the days of the pharaohs and again under the Persian king Darius; but most imports of spices, perfumes, pearls, and other luxuries moved from India and Arabia by land in their final passage to Syria or Egypt. In classical antiquity, until the last days of the Roman Empire, no truly major incursions or political pressures affected the Mediterranean enclave save for those exerted by the Persian empire and its successors in the Parthian and Sassanian dynasties.

Not only were the lands of ancient times bound together by water; they also shared a common "Mediterranean" climate that encouraged similar agricultural practices and patterns of human settlement. Still, it would be misleading to overemphasize either geographical or cultural uniformities. The Mediterranean was divided into a number of subsidiary seas: the Tyrrhenian or Sardinian west of Italy; the narrow Adriatic down which harsh winds often blew; the island-studded Aegean and others.[3] The peoples inhabiting these basins developed many different linguistic and cultural characteristics across the prehistoric era, many of which endured throughout ancient history. This chapter will consider the earliest stages to about 1000 B.C., and must rely—save for Syria and Egypt—on the physical evidence provided by archeological exploration. Such material often raises unanswerable questions, but it well illustrates maritime interconnections and may help to support the proposition advanced in the Introduction as to the fundamental requirements for the existence of true sea power.

The movement of physical objects within each basin can be traced far back into Neolithic times (down to about 3000). Obsidian from the island of Melos even appears on the Greek mainland in the preceding Mesolithic era; one can only speculate how knowledge of its availability was discovered and exploited in a period when Melos itself appears not to have been inhabited—were fishermen blown far offshore? To the north of Melos excavations on the island of Cythnos have revealed ties by the eighth and seventh millennia around the coasts of the Peloponnesus into the Adriatic.[4] Predynastic Egypt, in the fourth millennium, had established continuous relations with Syria, probably to gain the cedars of Lebanon which were still prized in historic times. By at least the third millennium interconnections between basins grew more noticeable, as in the appearance of objects made in the Cyclades as far as the Balearic islands and south France. Here too one can only guess what drew Aegean seafarers westward or why their products were acceptable in exchange for native items.

Across the second millennium, the height of the Bronze Age, physical objects, peoples, and even ideas moved about on a far larger scale, to the point that one can speak in terms of lines of trade. Egyptian gods were worshipped at Byblos, and the vessels that plied this route were called Byblos ships in hieroglyphic records. Economic ties led to political and military interventions by the powerful pharaohs of the Eighteenth Dynasty, culminating in the almost yearly invasions of Palestine and Syria by Thutmose III; in some of these his troops were transported by sea to avoid the arduous land march across the Sinai desert.

Particularly impressive was the swift progress of the inhabitants of the Aegean. Early in the second millennium the natives of Crete had advanced so far culturally that they could take the decisive step of creating civilized states, on the model of Syrian principalities, which were centered in the palaces of Cnossus, Phaestus, Kato Zakro, and elsewhere. Minoan civilization utilized scribes, writing in Linear A, to keep palace inventories and the like; its potters, ivory workers, and metal smiths produced magnificent artistic creations, which were attractive westward to the Lipari islands and other Tyrrhenian sites and eastward and south to Asia Minor, Syria, and Egypt; in Egyptian tombs of the era, opposite Luxor, exotic foreigners called Keftiu are pictured, who appear to be Minoans.

Objects of Minoan origin turn up widely in the Aegean itself, and what may be called colonies existed on the islands of Cythera and Thera, the latter ended by a violent eruption in the seventeenth century; then its fresco-decorated houses were buried under mounds of ash that have only recently been partially uncovered. The uncivilized lords of the mainland were also tempted by Minoan products, and the simple hillforts of Mycenae and elsewhere were embellished by true palaces that imitated Minoan ways by supporting scribes, fresco-painters, ivory workers, and other artisans and smiths.

The range of Mycenaean mariners stretched even farther afield than had that of Minoan merchants and raiders. At Scoglio del Tonno, a site on the heel of the Italian boot, so much Mycenaean pottery has been found that one may postulate a lasting settlement,[5] but Mycenaean vases turn up as far as Etruria, and a Mycenaean axe even in south England. The demand by Aegean craftsmen for amber also produced a regular route from the Baltic source down across central Europe to the Adriatic; once again one can only form hypotheses as to how the amber was passed from one set of hands to another and how knowledge of its existence was first attained.[6] Eastward Mycenaean settlement and acceptance of its wares are evident at several points on the coast of Asia Minor, Rhodes, Cyprus, Syria (particularly the site of Ras Shamra), and Egypt; in return eastern objects appear in Greece, such as Babylonian seals at inland Thebes.

Underwater archeology has of late been able to explore systematically a number of shipwrecks, especially along the coast of Asia Minor, which throw vivid light on aspects of this trade. A recent example, probably of the fourteenth century, at Ulu Burun opposite Rhodes had a varied cargo: 200 copper ingots of varying weight and shape along with tin and glass ingots; unworked elephant and hippopotamus ivory; gold and silver jewelry and medallions of Canaanite types and also a scarab of Nefertiti from Egypt; pottery of Cypriote, Mycenaean, and Syro-Palestinian origin; Babylonian objects; beads of faience, glass, and amber; myrrh or frankincense; figs and probably olive oil and wine—a traveling store indeed.[7] The excavators suggest that the voyage began on the Syrian coast but touched at Cyprus on its way to the Aegean, where perhaps the raw materials would have been traded for Mycenaean vases to be taken on to Egypt in a circular route.

The ship itself was a sailing vessel similar in construction to those of historic times. Reliefs at Deir el Bahri depict in great clarity the ship that Hatshepsut sent down the Red Sea to the fabled land of Punt; more sketchy representations on Minoan and Mycenaean seals also attest the use of ships with one mast and a big sail in the Aegean. Such vessels were undoubtedly small, like the caiques of historic times on to modern days. In the Mediterranean and Atlantic to the sixteenth century after Christ, as Braudel has demonstrated, ships were "little boats, mostly under 100 and even under 50 tons"; custom records in the Caribbean for the eighteenth century corroborate this picture.[8] Traders thus would need only limited capital; but even so how did the skipper of the Ulu Burun ship pay for his copper ingots from Cyprus or his tin and glass? Ports for such craft were no more than roadsteads.

Beside ships relying on sails, however, there were also rowed galleys of sleeker lines. On Minoan and Mycenaean seals five rowers at most are depicted, but ships on the Thera frescoes show an oarage of more than 20 on a side, and at least by Homeric times a complement of 50 rowers had become the standard.[9] The Mediterranean essentially lacks tides so that vessels of shallow draft could be drawn up on an open shore to rest the rowers at night; it also has very unreliable winds—Nelson, chasing Villeneuve in 1805, was delayed over a week off Sardinia.[10] Accordingly, methods of propulsion independent of external aid could have their advantages especially for piracy and coastal raids. The existence of the former scourge can only be presumed for the second millennium, but since it remained an endemic profession across Mediterranean history there is no reason to doubt that the question posed of strangers in the *Odyssey*, "Are you a pirate?" could have been put earlier. For coastal raids there is firmer evidence, both in Hittite complaints about attacks on Asia Minor coasts and in a fresco from Minoan Thera perhaps depicting an assault on a seacoast town; a similar raid is also shown on a silver vessel from Mycenae, of Minoan origin.[11] Oddly enough there has been serious effort to exculpate the "peace-loving" Minoans from any responsibility for nefarious marauding by sea; thus the commander in the Thera relief is asserted to have been Mycenaean even if in command of a Minoan crew.[12] We need not seek to rescue Minoan nobility by such tenuous arguments, though it is indeed quite likely that Mycenaean seafarers covered a wider zone in raiding as well as in trading.

What does this evidence on maritime activity especially in the second millennium have to do with the conscious utilization of sea power? The answer must be very little, and that has been my objective in surveying the archeological record in general outlines. Seaborne movement of physical objects in small vessels was not the dominant factor in economic life anywhere even if it provided the raw materials—metals, ivory, and so on—for craftsmen working for pharaohs, Syrian princelings, or Minoan and Mycenaean masters. Piracy and coastal raids were only incidental pinpricks on this trade, which suffered much more directly from sudden storms such as that which sank the Ulu Burun ship.

The only true example of control of adjacent waters for political and military purposes in the era was that exercised by the pharaohs of the Eighteenth Dynasty.[13] Already in the Old Kingdom of the third millennium troops had been transported by sea to Palestine; after the expulsion of the Hyksos invaders who had ended the Middle Kingdom the rulers who restored Egyptian unity, along with their followers, were more military minded than any other dynasty in Egyptian history. They pushed their power far up the Nile into Nubia, and used river craft to support their advance; as we saw earlier Thutmose III avoided in some of his campaigns in Palestine and Syria the march across the Sinai desert by ferrying his army by sea on vessels built in the royal dockyard near Memphis. These ships, however, were "only naval in that they were intended to serve the ends of war,"[14] for Thutmose III faced no opposition on the sea. He controlled all the Syrian ports, and no one else either could or desired to challenge Egyptian control of the eastern seaboard of the Mediterranean.

One famous "thalassocracy" does remain to be considered. In Greek legend a powerful king of Crete, called Minos, was active on the sea. Thucydides, more credulous of legend than one might expect, picked up the tale and in discussing the role of sea power in Greek history, proclaimed Minos the first to have a navy and went on to rationalize this power; Minos "from a natural desire to protect his growing revenues, sought, as far as he was able, to clear the sea of pirates." Clearly, Thucydides was transposing into the past the nature of Athenian naval imperialism in his own day. His predecessor Herodotus had been more critical; for him Polycrates, tyrant of Samos in the late sixth century, was the first to aim at empire of the sea, and he dismissed Minos as legendary.[15] But the weight of Thucydides' authority led to the acceptance of Minoan thalassocracy as a commonplace of ancient thought, and modern historians, also influenced consciously or unconsciously by Mahan and British naval power, have only rarely had any doubts. As a reasonably careful scholar recently put it, the Minoan fleet "was a navy that successfully policed the Mediterranean for centuries."[16]

The truth rather is that there is not one shred of positive evidence to support the myth of the Minoan thalassocracy, and much to weigh against its acceptance. In the greatest days of Minoan civilization Crete was divided into a number of principalities centered on the various palaces; this was no base for a major naval power. These palaces were unfortified, a fact often used to support the idea that they possessed a bulwark of wooden walls which could stand out to sea against invaders. Islands, however, commonly in history have relied on the sea itself to protect them against outside threats and so tend not to have navies of their own. The rulers of England only came to realize the necessity of meeting enemies on the sea rather than on the shore in the days of the Spanish Armada.[17]

If the Cretan states shared a navy, unlikely though that may be, it failed to protect them, for in the fifteenth century the island was invaded by Mycenaean warlords—who must have had their own ships. Thereafter the mainland Greek script of Linear B was used by the scribes of Cnossus, and a variety of other evidence attests this external mastery. Quite possibly the splendor of Cnossus in the period called Late Minoan II "was the result, not of far-ranging activities conducted by the fleet of an imperial Minos, but merely of the subjugation of all Crete to Knossian rule."[18] Finally, it may be observed that the galleys of the second millennium did not yet have rams with which to engage in battle by sea; they could have been used, as the Thera frescoes suggest, only for coastal raids.[19]

Toward the close of the Bronze Age Mediterranean lands suffered waves of invasion that in the west reached as far as Sicily in their devastation. Mycenaean palaces were sacked and burned in the period centering on 1200; Linear B was no longer needed because their bureaucracies were wiped out and life sank to as low a level as had been known for a thousand years or more. So too in Asia Minor the Hittite realm was overthrown, and other invaders marched down the coast of Syria by land and sea as far as Egypt. Here the Peoples of the Sea, as they are called in local records, were met just after 1200 by Ramses III, who

assembled "warships, galleys, and coasters . . . manned completely from bow to stern with valiant warriors carrying their
weapons."[20] The invaders were defeated in a great battle of
hand-to-hand combat with grappling irons, depicted later on his
temple at Medinet Habu.[21] This was the first known sea battle
in ancient history and the last for over half a millennium.

Egypt thus survived as a civilized state, but any naval power
it once had exercised vanished. In the eleventh century Wen
Amon from Karnak was sent to Byblos to purchase cedars of
Lebanon for the barque of Amon-Re; his gold and silver were
stolen in the town of Dor, and local princes showed little respect for his commission. Eventually, he did secure the timber,
but unfavorable winds carried him to Cyprus, where he met
further delays; then the papyrus account of his misadventures
breaks off, but it reveals both the continued trade of Egypt with
Phoenicia and the independent role of ships belonging to people
called Tjeker.[22] At the close of the Bronze Age as at its beginning the seas were open to maritime activity by anyone ven-
turing risks of storms and piracy, but mastery belonged to no
one power. Only in the next millennium were political and economic conditions to become so advanced and complex that a
variety of states were to seek naval dominion.

CHAPTER II

Prelude to Thalassocracy

The centuries immediately after 1000 B.C. are almost without history. Egypt continued to support its structure of government though it was often under alien rule; so too in Syria there were kingdoms on a minor scale, and also in Phoenicia small states centered on Tyre, Sidon, Byblos, and other ports. This era was the only period in ancient history in which the kingdom of David and Solomon could temporarily flourish. Civilization in the Aegean had totally disappeared, and even farmers were replaced in many areas by nomads. A new framework of life, nonetheless, was almost unconsciously arising, especially at Athens but also at other sites, which was to produce that political and cultural outlook we call Hellenic in distinction from the far different patterns of Mycenaean times.

By the eighth century the chaos of external invasions and internal disruptions had been overpassed, and progress became steadily more rapid and diversified in many significant aspects. In the age of expansion to 500 B.C., the focus of this chapter, the political, economic, and technological bases for potential thalassocracy were solidified in several stretches of the Mediterranean.

Commercially, Aramaeans, who used camels instead of donkeys, reopened lines of trade from Syria inland to Mesopotamia by the eighth century. With them came a host of luxury items in ivory, gold, and other metals produced by craftsmen in Phoenicia and Syria—not artistically of a high order though drawing in part on Egyptian prototypes yet skilled and attractive. As a consequence to some degree of the economic unification of the Near East, Assyrian monarchs created a large empire, though they had no interest in the sea beyond recording the submission of Cypriote rulers in boastful reports to their protective deity Ashur.

Equally important changes took place in the Mediterranean basin itself which swiftly bound together all its shores commercially and culturally. This was the result of Phoenician and Greek colonization in the eighth and following centuries.[1]

The Phoenicians had established themselves in Cyprus before 800 and pushed on westward, largely along the African coast, to the western part of Sicily, Sardinia, and Spain; their main strength, however, was in the area of modern Tunisia. Here Utica was reported to have been founded in the eleventh century and Kart-Hadasht or New Town, which we know as Carthage, was conventionally set at 814. But thus far probings at Carthage have produced no evidence of settlement before the later eighth century.[2]

Greek colonization in the western Mediterranean was probably as early as that of the Phoenicians. The first Greek outpost was established by Euboeans at Pithecusae on the island of Ischia to tap the metal resources of Etruia; a mixed population of Phoenicians and Syrians also inhabited this settlement.[3] Then followed a great outpouring in south Italy, eastern Sicily—where Syracuse was founded in 733—and southern France, especially at Massalia. Orthodoxy always distinguishes the two waves of western expansion by labeling Phoenician centers as trading posts and Greek colonies as purely agricultural, intended to export discontented elements of the homeland states, but this is too simplistic. The inhabitants of Carthage drew much of their wealth from the orchards and wheatfields of the hinterland, and it has become clear that while Greek settlers always had an eye to agricultural possibilities they were often preceded by the arrival of Aegean traders and that they spread among native populations Greek wares as "intermediaries between the professional traders and markets of Greece and a quite different economic pattern among their barbarian neighbours."[4] The colonists themselves desired objects manufactured in Greek workshops and thus fostered the rise of true urban centers at Corinth, Athens, and elsewhere by 600.[5]

Whereas the Aegean in 1000 had been an isolated enclave with very limited contacts to the Near East and its inhabitants had no real knowledge of surrounding seas—as the legendary travels of much-suffering Odysseus attest—commercial connections between colonies and homeland now produced a spiderweb of ties; every pressure or intrusion from outside affected to some degree the whole of the Greek world. "Greece lies scattered in many regions," as a later orator rightly observed.[6] Interest in the sea also naturally evolved. Odysseus could dream of taking his oar so far inland that people would not know what it was; there he might dwell in peace. Late in the eighth century Hesiod gives some advice on the proper season for trading by sea "though I have no skill in seafaring nor in ships," but boasts that his only trip by sea was from mainland Aulis to Chalcis (the modern bridge here is 164 feet long).[7] As the later poet Aratus looked back he well expressed this point of view:

> The hurt of strife they knew not in their day,
> Nor yet sharp quarrel and the noise of war.
> Simply they lived, the rude sea far away,
> No ships to bring their living from afar;
> But cows and ploughs and Justice in her rule
> Freely gave all, of just gifts bountiful.[8]

By 600, however, Alcaeus had created the lasting metaphor of "the ship of state," and the sea became more deeply imbedded in Greek awareness, though it must be observed that most Greeks never went to sea and feared its dangers.[9] Those who did venture abroad supported an ever more lively and vital commerce in textiles, timber, bulk metals and manufactured wares, agricultural products, slaves, and pottery—not an extensive range, true, but then Greek industrial life was of a very simple order that did not need many of the raw and finished items moving in trade nowadays. By 500, even so, cities such as Corinth, Athens, Miletus, and other coastal ports were dependent at least in part on seaborne grain, coming down the Hellespont from south Russia, Sicily, and also from Egypt.[10]

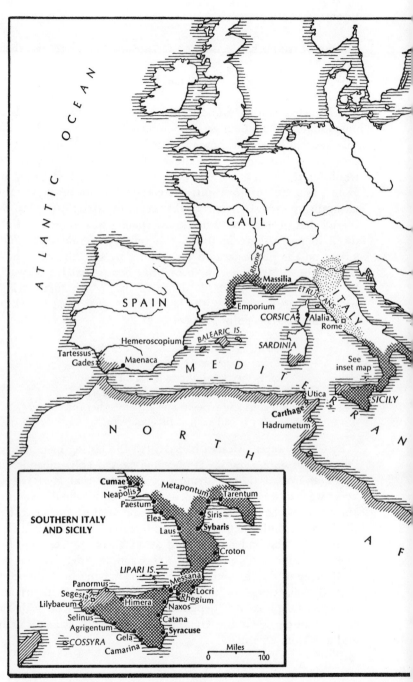

ATLANTIC OCEAN

GAUL

Rhone R.

Massilia

SPAIN

Emporium

ETRUSCANS

CORSICA •Alalia
Rome

ITALY

Hemeroscopium

BALEARIC IS.

SARDINIA

See
inset map

Tartessus
Gades •Maenaca

M E D I T E R R A N E A N

•Utica

Carthage
Hadrumetum

SICILY

N O R T H

A
F

**SOUTHERN ITALY
AND SICILY**

Cumae
Neapolis

Metapontum

•Paestum

Elea

Laus

Siris

Sybaris

Tarentum

Croton

LIPARI IS.

Panormus

Segesta

Lilybaeum

Messana
Locri
Rhegium

Selinus

Himera

Naxos

Agrigentum

Catana

Syracuse

COSSYRA

Gela

Camarina

Miles

0   100

18

MAP 8
EXPANSION OF GREEK CIVILIZATION
750 B.C.-500 B.C.

Greek   Phoenician   Other

Scale of Miles

0   500

CASPIAN SEA

Olbia
Tyras
Theodosia
Istrus
Chersonesus   Phasis
Danube R.
BLACK SEA
Mesembria   Sinope
Apollonia
Epidamnus   Amisus   Trapezus
Byzantium   Heraclea
Corcyra   Chalcedon   URARTU
Cyzicus
PHRYGIA
Megara   Chalcis   Phocaea   Nineveh
Corinth   Eretria   LYDIA   ASSYRIAN
ACHAEA   Miletus   Aspendus   EMPIRE
IONIA   PAMPHYLIA   CILICIA
Rhodes   Al Mina
CRETE   CYPRUS
E   A   N   S   E   A   Tyre   Babylon
PHOENICIA
Cyrene
Barca   Naucratis
LIBYA
Memphis
E   G   Y   P   T
R   I   C   A
RED SEA
Nile R.

19

When terms such as commerce and trade enter our text we touch on a major area of debate among students of ancient economic life, especially in its early stages. A view that commands wide assent argues that at this point one should think in terms of "gift exchange" among aristocrats, after Marcel Mauss's famous *Le Don,* rather than deliberate trade for profit. In the rise of prehistoric sea voyaging this interpretation may have its merit, but by early in the first millennium a variety of evidence suggests that it is too restrictive. In the *Odyssey* Phoenician merchants are busy in the Aegean, and Odysseus himself pretends to be a trader seeking profit (*kerdos*).[11] The vigorous expansion of Greek seafaring in the eighth and seventh centuries is unlikely to have occurred unless the traders of the era expected gain to compensate for the risks of piracy and storm. Herodotus casually comments thus on Colaeus of Samos, who was blown to Tartessus in Spain but turned the misadventure into producing a great profit.[12] With respect to another very common argument, that trade of any type was restricted to luxuries, the evidence for movement of many forms of raw materials—wool, timber, metal, grain, and so on—is irrefutable.

The Father of History also has an amusing tale of Carthaginians dealing with a native population somewhere on the Atlantic coast of Africa; they laid out objects on the shore, and the natives came down with gold. If the Carthaginians did not consider the exchange fair they so indicated, and only when both sides were satisfied could trade take place.[13] As this story suggests, there was in simple conditions no standard measure of value; instead the Homeric world evaluated objects in heads of cattle (as when Glaucus and Diomedes exchanged gilded for bronze armor, "the price of a hundred oxen for nine"), cauldrons, iron spits, and similar objects.[14] By 600 Greek states were commencing to adopt the Lydian innovation of stamped and uniform nuggets of precious metal, true coins, a development that spread like wildfire over homeland and colonies alike and did at last produce an easily assessed standard of valuation.

Economically, to sum up a very general treatment of major advances, a foundation for potential thalassocracy had been laid by 500 in an awareness of the importance of seaborne commerce.

The growth of trade and industry as well as the appearance of true markets in the nascent cities for the sale of agricultural products much increased the wealth of the Greek states, and the use of coinage in silver made that wealth more easily tapped for the construction of costly warships.

No significant changes took place in the sailing ships that carried this trade. Vessels remained small, built on trim lines like the modern caiques of the Aegean and equipped with one mast and a square sail of hides stitched together.[15] Tacking accordingly could be executed only in a limited degree, and ships tended to hug the coasts so that they could run ashore to escape a major storm—though the evidence of shipwrecks shows that they were not always successful. By 500 there were far more sailing ships and the infrastructure of trade was being improved. Moles and other harbor works were constructed at major ports, though Athens still used the open roadstead of Phalerum for its exports of pottery; at the isthmus of Corinth a slipway (*diolkos*) had been built by 600 so that cargoes could avoid the dangerous voyage around the southern promontories of the Peloponnesus, probably mainly marble west to Delphi and timber eastward to the states of the Saronic Gulf.[16] Shippers could also now make use of coastal guides, written by Hecataeus and others.[17]

The remarkable development in marine architecture concerned warships. In the early centuries of the first millennium the standard galley was the pentekonter, so called because it had 50 oarsmen, 25 on a side. This vessel had its main utility in piracy and in coastal raids; it also had advantages for long voyages into unknown waters, where the manpower of the crew might help to protect a vessel against local threats.[18] In the *Odyssey* the hero sacked a Thracian city, "killed the men and, taking the women and plenty of cattle and goods, divided them up."[19] Athenian vases of the eighth century depict galleys bent on similar missions, and dedications of booty gained in raids began to appear in Greek sanctuaries.[20]

The important alteration was the addition of a bronze ram at the prow of a pentekonter. Although a Corinthian vase early in the seventh century may depict a ram, the first literary reference to its use in battle is in 535 off Alalia.[21] Full use of the ram re-

quired an increase in the power with which a galley was propelled, but this presented problems. The great Athenian ship
storage buildings of the fourth century allowed for galleys no
more than 35 by 8 meters,[22] and it was not technically possible
to construct purely wooden vessels that were much longer—in
heavy seas, when a ship might be supported only on prow and
stern by waves, the midship section could take only a limited
amount of stress. The solution seems to have been reached in
Phoenicia; an Assyrian relief of *c.* 690 already shows a Phoenician ship with a ram and two banks of oars.[23] Thucydides as-
cribes the first appearance of the new type in Greece to a Corinthian shipwright in the seventh century, a view which accords ill
with the fact that such warships entered service only in the later
sixth century; the first literary reference to the trireme occurs in
the satirical poetry of Hipponax, conventionally dated *c.* 540.
According to Thucydides, most Greek fleets before the Persian
wars were composed of pentekonters.[24]

Essentially, the solution consisted of fitting three oarsmen in
the space allotted to one on a pentekonter. This produced the
trireme or in Greek *triere,* the major galley of the classic period,
with a crew of 170 oarsmen plus a deck crew and marines numbering about 30 as a rule.[25] Just how the rowers in each group
of three were arranged has been the subject of a long debate.
Down into the twentieth century classical scholars visualized the
rowers as stacked one above another; in a version of *Ben Hur*
filmed in the 1920's the galley was so constructed, with the result that a launch out of sight of the camera had to tow it, for
the rowers could not manipulate their oars, necessarily of very
different lengths. More recently, a system that tucks the oarsmen
into groups ranging inboard and only slightly higher in each
tier has been generally accepted as being practicable and also
fitting the ancient evidence. To reduce the weight as much as
possible the trireme had no ballast (so that it would float even if
holed in battle); a galley could capsize if all the crew ran to one
side of the vessel.[26] Normally it carried a very limited amount of
food and water; Thucydides notes as an exception the fact that
the Corinthian fleet off Corcyra in 432 had three days' food.[27]

A trireme is better compared to a racing shell than to a battleship. Its crew could reach a speed of seven knots for short spurts, but fleets usually cruised at no more than two knots, then often aided by one big sail that could be lowered in battle.[28] The bottom oarports were not far above the water line, though they could be fitted with leather masks;[29] if bad weather arose, warfleets had to make for shore, and always they remained close to land so that they could rest and feed their crews in greater comfort at night. In antiquity a blockade of an enemy port was not easy unless the blockaders had a friendly base nearby; during the civil war between Caesar and Pompey the admiral Bibulus sought to contain Caesar's reenforcements under Antony at Brundisium, but his crews had to drink dew to get their water and the blockade failed. When Antony did slip out, Pompeian galleys gave chase to the sailing ships, but "suddenly the wind sprang up stronger than before, filled their great sails unexpectedly, and enabled them to complete their voyage without fear. The pursuers were left behind and they suffered severely from the wind and waves in the narrow sea and were scattered along a harborless and rocky coast."[30] Warships, in other words, could not go faster than sailing ships with a good wind, though we do hear from time to time of their preying on merchantmen.[31]

Why did the Greeks uniformly adopt such a restricted instrument of naval warfare? One must be reminded of their settling on an apparently equally peculiar choice of formation in land warfare, the close-packed mass of infantrymen in the phalanx, which the Persian general Mardonius was to ridicule as useful only in straight encounters on flat land.[32] But just as there were solid reasons for the dominance of the phalanx, so too the trireme was admirably adapted to its primary function, battle at sea, "an entirely new kind of craft, one that was, in effect, a man-driven torpedo armed with a pointed cutwater for puncturing an enemy hull."[33] Powered as it was by oarsmen, it was precisely maneuverable to sheer along the side of another warship, snapping off its oars, and then turning to ram a vulnerable stern. Ramming, indeed, was dangerous prow to prow; in the battle of Alalia the Phocaeans lost 40 ships in battle and of the 20 remaining the "beaks were so bent and blunted as to be no longer serviceable."[34] By the fifth century the Athenians in particular had become much more proficient in naval tactics, which were summed up by the admiral Phormio in an address to his men in the Gulf of Corinth:

> One cannot sail up in the proper way to make an attack by ramming, unless one has a good long view of the enemy, nor can one back away at the right moment if one is hard pressed oneself; it is impossible also to sail through the enemy's line and then wheel back on him—which are the right tactics for the fleet which has the superior seamanship. Instead of all this, one would be compelled to fight a naval action as though it were a battle on land, and under those circumstances the side with the greater number of ships has the advantage.[35]

His two subsequent victories over the Corinthians are almost unique in naval history inasmuch as they were won primarily by maneuver.[36]

The advantages of a galley for warfare made it the warship par excellence all across ancient history and on through medieval Venetian and other navies; still in the late eighteenth century the Russians had a fleet of galleys in the Black Sea, which John Paul Jones commanded for a time. Not until gunpowder had made its appearance and sailing ships could be equipped with cannon as floating platforms for attack from a distance did the galley lose its utility. Since triremes, despite Phormio's preference for maneuver, did often close in for hand-to-hand combat they were not only provided with a limited number of archers, javelin throwers, and marines, but also the rowers might have to engage in the fray.[37] Accordingly, oarsmen were always free men in antiquity and medieval times; slaves or convicts could be used only in times of emergency.[38]

Economically, as noted earlier, the progress of the Aegean world by 500 rested on waterborne commerce in a variety of commodities, including grain, and it had grown much wealthier. Now an instrument of naval warfare had been fashioned that could be utilized to secure command of the seas if a state had access to proper timber supplies and hemp (for the girding cables that helped hold a trireme together). The average Greek state, however, numbered no more than a population of a thousand, and could at best have only one or two warships.[39] Creating a navy, manning its vessels, and replacing worn-out warships at least every 20 years required the resources and manpower of much larger communities such as Athens, Corinth, or Sparta; and even then some form of pooling of interstate resources was almost essential for any Greek strength on the seas.[40]

By the closing decades of the sixth century two other areas of the Mediterranean had progressed politically or economically to be able to support navies from their own wealth, and also had reason to do so. When the Phoenician coast came under the control first of the Assyrians and then the Persians, the settlements in the western Mediterranean were cast adrift, if indeed they had ever been supervised by Tyre and Sidon. Cultural connections remained so strong that after the Persian king Cambyses conquered Egypt and wished to use Phoenician ships to extend his power westward to Carthage he met a flat refusal "to war on their own children,"[41] but politically mastery of the network of Phoenician outposts in Africa, Sicily, Sardinia, and Spain was acquired by Carthage at least by the sixth century. This vast trading empire produced extensive profits in gold, silver, and other objects; to support their control the Carthaginians created the first true thalassocracy in ancient times, and deliberately sent exploratory missions in the Atlantic Ocean down the African coast and up as far as Britain.

We know little about how its fleet was organized save that the inner of the two harbors at Carthage was the military port, nor can we guess its size. Apart from a very doubtful battle with Massalia about 600 the only known naval conflict is that against the Phocaean colony at Alalia in Corsica in 535, and even though the Carthaginians joined forces with the Etruscans they were defeated; the Greeks, however, had eventually to retreat to Elea on the Italian coast. Carthage, even so, had a reputation for being ruthless with all foreign ships invading its preserves, and repelled the effort of the Spartan Dorieus to found a colony in Libya. There is a fair amount of testimony to piracy in the early western Mediterranean, especially by Etruscans and the natives of the Lipari islands, but one may presume that Carthaginian strength limited their preying on trade mainly to Italian waters.[42]

The Greek colonies in Sicily were too divided politically to mount a unified threat on the sea; the Etruscan states might have done so but were generally on good terms with the Carthaginians.[43] The Carthaginian fleet thus need not have been a large force, especially since it was backed by skillful diplomatic activity. From the first years of the Roman Republic (508–7) there survived to the days of Polybius a treaty in which the Romans agreed essentially to trade only with Carthage, Sardinia, and western Sicily, a treaty renewed in 348. That its provisions were respected is proved by the fact that at the later date pottery made in Rome was exported only to the regions in question but not farther in Africa.[44]

The other area was the Persian empire. The Persians were landlubbers, as Herodotus noted;[45] but they were aggressive in expanding their empire and strong enough to master any adjacent waters. Darius extended Persian rule into northwest India "and made use of the sea [i.e., the Persian Gulf] in those parts."[46] When he invaded Scythia the Ionians had to provide ships with which to bridge the Hellespont and protect his communications. The Persian monarchs also relied on the naval strength of the Phoenicians. To invade Egypt Cambyses expanded his naval strength greatly beyond the resources that the Phoenicians could furnish; by 500 the Persians had 200 warships on hand for the tyrant of Miletus in his promise to subjugate the Aegean islands. As we shall see in the next chapter, Persian naval mastery of the eastern Mediterranean was not to be challenged until Xerxes' invasion of Greece in 480–79.

The political structure of the Greek world itself had matured across the age of expansion to produce the fully developed *polis,* a body of citizens united in common worship of a patron divinity and equipped with a well-organized pattern of government that could levy harbor tolls and other fees to tap the growing wealth of their ports. The major *poleis* along the Aegean shores had come to rely, as already noted, on imports of metals, grain, and so on, which were matched by exports of manufactured wares. The island state of Aegina was particularly active in the transport of grain from south Russia down the Hellespont, which the refugee Histaeus of Miletus blockaded briefly in 494; it was not accidental that Aegina was also prominent in putting down piracy, as in the case of Samian exiles at Cretan Cydonia, who tried to attack trade to Egypt. Corinth played a similar role in the Adriatic and had a fleet of some 70 ships by the end of the sixth century. Thucydides' sketch of early Greek history measures its advance in terms of increasing use of the sea, and Thucydides even asserts that navies to the outbreak of the Persian wars "were still a great source of strength . . . they brought in revenue and they were the foundation of empire. . . . There was no warfare on land that resulted in the acquisition of an empire. What wars there were were simply frontier skirmishes."[47]

This is a fascinating example, the first in Western literature, of the distorted role assigned to sea power, for the political and military conflicts of Greek states by land actually had a very important result, the mastery by Sparta of all the Peloponnesus save for Argos. Sparta had no desire to extend its power farther, partly because it always needed to keep an eye on its helots, who revolted more than once, and by the end of the sixth century had formed a league of its dependent allies, who had their own assembly and a voice in general decisions. The Greek world often turned to Sparta for counsel and protection; in particular it was to give invaluable leadership when the Persians invaded Greece, for the Spartans stood firmly against any external threat or internal aggression.

In view of the conventional view of Sparta as conservative and land-locked it may appear surprising that in the sixth century Sparta was one of the most active Greek states on the sea; when it had occasion to intervene in Athens to expel the Pisistratid dynasty the army of Cleomenes came by sea and met no resistance in landing at Phalerum. Once it even reached its power across the Aegean to attack Polycrates of Samos, though unsuccessfully. Polycrates, tyrant *c.* 540–22, was according to Herodotus the first man consciously to try to exercise naval mastery.[48] He began active piratical campaigns with a fleet of pentekonters, and then moved on to build the far more complicated and expensive triremes. Eventually the Persians tricked him into coming to the mainland, where they seized and crucified him.

The Greek state that was advancing most rapidly in the economic sphere in the sixth century was Athens. Its urban focus became steadily larger and was embellished by Pisistratus and his sons; one of these, Hippias, enticed the poet Anacreon fron Cnidus by sending a warship—a pentekonter—to fetch him, and otherwise supported arts and letters.[49] Athenian potters developed first the famed black-figure style of vases and then by the last quarter of the sixth century the red-figure style; by this time they had driven Corinthian and Laconian rivals out of the market all over the Mediterranean. The wares of one Athenian potter, Nicosthenes, have been found in south Russia, Egypt, and Etruria; and for the latter patrons Nicosthenes made vases in Etruscan shapes and decorated with myths appealing to the Etruscans.[50] Potters, smiths, and other inhabitants of bustling Athens ate seaborne grain as much as Milesians or Ephesians did.

Yet Athens played an insignificant role on the sea until 500. Its vases in the eighth century, one may recall, depicted galleys engaged in coastal raids, and there was a formal structure of naucraries, coastal districts, which were obligated to provide warships much like the English Cinque Ports.[51] Nonetheless, the fleet that could be assembled was totally inadequate to cope with the naval strength of Aegina, a few miles across the Saronic Gulf, though Athens and Aegina were very commonly at odds. In their greatest conflict before 500 the Athenians were so weak that they bought 20 ships from Corinth to make up a total of 70, which won an initial naval battle, but then the Aeginetans fell on the Athenians in disorder and routed them.[52] The first reference to Athenian triremes comes only at the end of the sixth century; it even appears probable that the 20 ships the Athenians sent to Ionia in 498 were still pentekonters.[53]

Much later, in the Peloponnesian War, the Syracusan leader Hermocrates observed that "in fact the Athenians were more landsmen than the Syracusans and had only taken to the sea when forced to do so by the Persians."[54] Accidents can have mighty effects in shaping the course of history. Yet while the expansion of Athens in the sixth century may have psychologically paved the way for the remarkable developments to follow, it remains true that in 500 the Carthaginians were dominant by sea in the western Mediterranean and the Persians in eastern waters.

CHAPTER III

Athens on the Sea

In 499 the Greek states on the western seaboard of Asia Minor rebelled against their Persian overlord and sent the Milesian leader Aristagoras to implore the aid of Sparta, the balance wheel of the Greek state system which usually answered cries of help. Unfortunately he made the mistake of showing a map of the world, a novel invention to the Spartans; when they discovered that the Persian capital was a three-month march inland they bade him be gone by nightfall, and his efforts to bribe king Cleomenes failed. At Athens, on the other hand, the envoy secured the support of the nascent Athenian democracy; Herodotus wryly deduced that "it seems indeed to be easier to deceive a multitude than one man." The Athenians sent 20 warships and Eretria added four. Herodotus accounted this aid which helped the rebels sack the Persian regional center of Sardis but then was withdrawn "the beginnings of ills for the Greeks and barbarians alike";[1] in another light it may be reckoned the first of a train of events that were to lead to remarkable results.

After initial successes the Ionian rebels had to face the full might of the Persians, who like all empires took time to assemble their forces, including a fleet provided by the Phoenician ports. For the first time in Aegean history the decisive turning point was a sea battle; off Lade in 495 the League navy was defeated when many of the Greek ships retreated.[2] Miletus was taken early in the next year and was destroyed as an object lesson. To punish the Athenians for their aid, a small amphibious force was despatched in 490 straight across the Aegean. The Athenians dared

not try to meet it on the sea even though it was encumbered by
horse transports, but at Marathon on the east coast of Attica
they secured a great victory by land. The Spartans, who had
promised assistance, were delayed by a religious festival and arrived only after the battle was over, to marvel at the Persian
dead. For the first time the Greek world could venture to feel
that the Medes, as the Persians were often called, were not invincible.[3]

Then Darius died, and his son Xerxes had to spend several
years consolidating his rule before he could return to the Greek
problem; the Persian empire had many frontiers in Asia and
Africa, and its leaders probably considered the Greeks as no
more than a minor set of far-off barbarians, divided in internal
friction. This time Xerxes majestically decided to lead the expedition himself to gain military glory. So a huge army and navy,
twice the size of any force the Greeks could field, was assembled
in Asia Minor during the fall of 481.

By this time two events had taken place at Athens; one might
even say that the goddess Athena had worked two miracles for
her favorite *polis*. The first was the discovery of a very rich lode
in the state silver mines of Laurium. Normally the revenues were
divided among the citizen body, but such was not to be the case
this time. Second, Themistocles had become undisputed leader
of Athens by ostracizing his opponents; praised by Thucydides
as a man who "could best divine what was likely to happen in
the remotest future," he persuaded his fellow citizens to expend
the money on building the first major Athenian fleet, 200 triremes in all, and to begin fortifying the port of Piraeus as a base.
As Thucydides sums up his policy, "It was he who first ventured
to tell the Athenians that their future was on the sea."[4] One can
only speculate as to how so many ships could be built in a short
space of time and whence the timber and hemp were secured.[5]
The four-drachma coins struck in great profusion by the Athenians at this point were among the most poorly designed ever to
be issued by a Greek mint, and the ships must have been an
equally scratch job even though Themistocles insisted on a
sleek and maneuverable design.[6]

Still, these ships were to be the salvation of Greece; "the fate of Hellas depended on her navy," as Athenian envoys later reminded the Spartans.[7] The Greek states that refused to surrender were only a small fraction of the multitude of mainland *poleis*, but they drew the proper lesson from the earlier dissensions of the Ionian rebels and concentrated command by land and by sea in the hands of Spartan leaders. In the spring of 480 they met at the isthmus of Corinth to concert their resistance. The Peloponnesians insisted on building a wall across the isthmus itself, a naïve plan that quite overlooked the fact that the Persian fleet could outflank its defense and the likelihood that Argos, which had remained neutral out of hostility to Sparta, would join the Persians as soon as they drew near.

Themistocles analyzed matters quite differently. The Persian army numbered perhaps 180,000 men (Herodotus gives the incredible figure of 1,700,000), but its lightly equipped battalions were no match in open battle with the disciplined phalanxes of Greek spearsmen. On the sea conditions were less favorable. The Persian navy had over 600 warships; the backbone consisted of the Phoenician contingents, far more skilled in rowing techniques than the Greeks. Yet there was a serious weakness in the Persian plan of invasion, which Themistocles' keen mind spotted. The army was so large that it had to move close to the shore to receive seaborne grain; the navy in turn hugged the coast to protect the supply vessels. If only the Greeks could defeat the Persian navy, Xerxes' army would be a less serious threat. To secure the proper conditions for naval victory two steps were necessary. The maritime powers among the Greek allies, especially Athens, must concentrate all their energies on the sea; and then the Greek admirals must inveigle the superior Persian navy into narrow waters where its numbers and the skill of the Phoenician galleys would be less effective. By dextrous argument Themistocles secured agreement that the Greeks would send their naval forces north with a small army to delay and, if possible, cripple the enemy.

At first the Greeks selected the vale of Tempe in northern Thessaly as a suitable line of defense but discovered that the position could be turned if the Persians made a short inland detour. Accordingly, they fell back to Thermopylae, where the coastal road was hemmed between sea and mountains to a path only 50 feet wide; the other routes from Thessaly south into Boeotia lay so far inland that the Persian strategic necessity of keeping army and navy together prevented their use. Off Thermopylae lay the island of Euboea, which would force the Persian navy to come into a narrow strait; to block its entry the Greek fleet anchored at the northern end of the strait at Artemisium, while a minor detachment guarded its southern exit. Since this was a delaying position, limited forces were committed by land. The Spartan king Leonidas led 300 Spartan elite with allies to total some 9000 men; the Spartan admiral Eurybiades, however, had most of the Athenian and other naval contingents, numbering 271 triremes in the main fleet.

The mighty panoply of Xerxes made its way slowly across the Hellespont via two bridges of boats; along the north coast of the Aegean, where a canal had been dug for his fleet across the dangerous Mt. Athos peninsula, and down into Greece. Everywhere the native peoples and states surrendered. As Xerxes approached Thermopylae, his fleet encountered a violent storm that raged three days and sank many ships; the Greek forces, in the sheltered lee of Euboea, were not damaged. The enemy navy suffered further damage when Xerxes sent a large detachment around Euboea to bottle up the Greek fleet, for another storm blew the 200 Persian ships of this flotilla onto the rocks of the island.

The main fleet then fought three battles with the Greeks off Artemisium, in which neither side could secure a decisive victory. While his fleet was trying to force a passage by sea, Xerxes also launched an attack by land at the defenders of the narrow pass of Thermopylae. For two days his Persian "Immortals" died in droves before the stern Greek lines; but on the second night a local traitor revealed the existence of a trail up the mountains behind the Greeks. The movement of the Persian flanking force was detected by Leonidas in time to send off most of his army; he and his Spartans sacrificed themselves to delay the main Persian thrust. The Greek navy had no recourse but to retreat to the island of Salamis, off Attica.

The Greeks could gain comfort from their success in whittling down the enemy navy, yet as their council of war met on the shore of Salamis they could see smoke spiraling up from the Athenian Acropolis, where the Persians had quickly overcome the resistance of the priests and set fire to the temple roofs. All other Athenians had abandoned their homes and were now on the island of Salamis or at Troezen in the Peloponnesus.

Some of the Greek admirals wished to withdraw to the isthmus of Corinth and anchor off its wall. Themistocles argued forcefully that the only Greek hope lay in sticking to the main line of strategy of naval action and in response to a taunt that he no longer had a country or a right to speak threatened to sail off with the Athenian ships and citizens to found a new state in the western Mediterranean. Since all realized the Greeks had no chance without the strong Athenian navy, they yielded once more to his keen analysis and agreed to hold their position. So both sides remained indecisive, for Xerxes could not settle whether to advance by land on the isthmus of Corinth or deal with the Greek naval forces off his flank.

As dissensions arose again in the Greek naval command, the wily Themistocles took the dangerous course of sending by night a trusted slave, Sicinnus, to the Persians to tell Xerxes that the Greeks were quarreling, that the Athenians were willing to turn traitor, and that if he wanted a great victory he needed only to attack. Xerxes fell into the trap and ordered his fleet to advance for the final blow; to make victory doubly sure he sent a detachment around to the west end of the strait to bottle up the Greeks. He himself sat upon a throne on a hill overlooking the battleground so that he could award prizes to the most valorous of his subjects.

On a morning in late September the Persian fleet, now reduced to some 350 ships, rowed in line abreast from its anchorage on the Attic shore toward Salamis. The Greeks, who had about 300 ships in the action, knew that they were encircled from the rear and prepared for the decisive battle; Athenian hoplites were embarked on the ships. As the Persians closed in, their line was split by the little island of Psyttalia; the resulting confusion was heightened by the apparent retreat of the Greeks, who backed water on seeing the Persians enter the narrow reaches of the bay.

This tactical maneuver, however, was designed only to suck the enemy farther in; suddenly the Greeks rowed forward from front and flanks and threw themselves into hand-to-hand battle with the Persians, who had no chance to use maneuvering tactics. By the close of the day the despondent Xerxes could see his remaining ships rowing away in utter defeat. Some 200 Persian warships, mostly of the Phoenician contingent, were lost, as against only about 40 Greek ships.

Xerxes struck his tents and returned speedily to Asia Minor. Since the Persians could no longer be sure of supplies by sea, he also took back much of his army. As has usually been the case in history, the proper use of sea power can facilitate victory, but the final step must come by land. In the next year (479) at Plataea the allied army under Spartan command was equal in strength to the Persian force and routed it in a very untidy battle.

Salamis made possible the almost unbelievable Greek deliverance, and Themistocles was the indomitable agent to help engineer the success. True, others had a hand in the glorious days of 480–79: the Spartans provided leadership, which the allies accepted without demur; after the battle of Salamis it was the Aeginetans who got first prize for their role. The Athenians did not have sufficient manpower for all their warships by themselves; at Artemisium they provided 127 galleys, but some were rowed by Plataeans, and 20 by men from Chalcis. At Salamis all 200 were present, but again Chalcis manned 20.[8] Even so, Herodotus' judgment was sound:

> At this point I find myself compelled to express an opinion which I know most people will object to; nevertheless, as I believe it to be true, I will not suppress it. If the Athenians, through fear of the approaching danger, had abandoned their country, or if they had stayed there and submitted to Xerxes, there would have been no attempt to resist the Persians by sea; and in the absence of a Greek fleet, it is easy to see what would have been the course of events on land. . . . It was the Athenians who—after God—drove back the Persian king.[9]

So too it was the Athenians who were to capitalize on the Greek success by moving steadily if unintentionally to consolidate the first great thalassocracy, one of the most productive and important in Western history. In this development Themistocles, the initial *fons et origo,* played no part; he soon fell victim himself to the bitter fights of Athenian politics and eventually wound up a pensioner of the Persian king in Asia Minor.

The Spartans, having done their duty in 480–79, were ready to stop; to counter the strong possibility that the Persians would regroup their strength, as they had in the Ionian revolt, the Spartans suggested simply moving the people of the cities on the coast of Asia Minor to the Greek mainland. The Ionians were reluctant to leave the homes and graves of their ancestors, and Athens stepped forward, willing to serve as the leader in taking revenge on the Persians and securing the liberty of the Aegean states. As Thucydides put it, the Spartans "were anxious to be rid of the war against the Medes. They thought that the Athenians were capable of undertaking the leadership and that at that time they were well disposed towards them." This may be too simple, but the Spartans did have enough troubles at home to keep them preoccupied, and political direction at Athens by this point had passed to the aristocrat Cimon, a pro-Spartan figure.[10]

A number of Asiatic and island states met at the sacred island of Delos in the summer of 477 and formed a league; each state was to provide warships or, in the case of smaller states, cash to help defray the expenses of war. Leadership was voluntarily assigned to Athens, which would furnish admirals (and the largest fleet), treasurers, and presidents of the league assembly. In flamboyant fashion the allies threw lumps of iron into the sea and swore to remain united until the iron floated; but in reality none of them probably expected lasting military involvement. As a modern historian succinctly observed, "What they had neglected to stipulate was the time for which they were to remain allies."[11]

Athens duly marshalled Greek strength to sweep the Persians out of the Aegean and then the south coast of Asia Minor, also largely occupied by Greek states; the greatest triumph was the destruction by Cimon of the renascent Persian fleet at the battle of the Eurymedon river, early in the 460's. By this time the nature of the league was subtly altering. When the small state of Carystus on the island of Euboea had been liberated, it was then, against its will, forced to join the league; the crusade must not be weakened by local unwillingness to participate. Soon the island of Naxos grew weary of the annual burden of providing ships, but Athens quickly compelled it to resume its role in the common effort. Worst of all was the "revolt" of Thasos, a large state, in 465, which had to be recalled to its fealty by a siege. Voluntary league, in sum, slowly, almost unconsciously, was becoming empire. Modern students date the point at which the process was complete to 454, when the treasury of the league, safeguarded at the temple of Apollo on Delos, was moved to Athens, where Athena and her priests could better protect it on the Acropolis in the event of a sudden Persian foray into the Aegean.

This peculiar pattern of imperialism does not accord neatly with modern theories of the rise of imperialist powers as explicable entirely in economic terms. Hobson, the fountainhead of this view, who was followed by Lenin, built his thesis almost entirely on the career of Cecil Rhodes, a very untypical example of English expansion; perhaps we should keep in mind an alternative explanation. Schumpeter, for instance, described the rise of the Persian empire as a good illustration of the ambition of upper classes throughout history; a recent powerful assessment of Roman imperialism by W. V. Harris attributes Roman conquests to an "ideology of *laus* and *gloria*" among the leading Roman families and only secondarily to the profits gained from victory.[12] To return to Athens, the main objective driving the Athenians was, in the words of Jacqueline de Romilly, "the desire which they have for fame, renown, and honours. In its highest form, their ambition aims at glory, in its lowest at the use of power."[13]

Financial profit was an incidental by-product, though Athenian leaders were well aware that their mastery could be used economically for political purposes, and in particular they controlled by means of Hellespontophylakes, or guards of the Hellespont, the import of Russian grain by other states. One of the first salvoes in the events leading to the outbreak of the Peloponnesian War in 431 was the Megarian decree of the Athenian assembly, under the instigation of Pericles, which

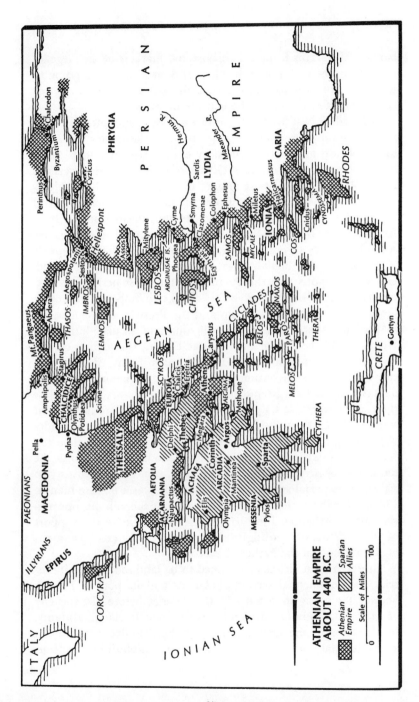

ATHENIAN EMPIRE
ABOUT 440 B.C.

Athenian
Empire

Spartan
Allies

Scale of Miles
0   100

ITALY

IONIAN SEA

CORCYRA

EPIRUS

ILLYRIANS

PAEONIANS

MACEDONIA

Pella

Pydna

THESSALY

Mt. Pangaeus

Amphipolis

Stagirus

CHALCIDICE

Olynthus

Potidaea

Scione

Abdera

THASOS

IMBROS

LEMNOS

SCYROS

Aegospotami

Sestos

Hellespont

Perinthus

Byzantium

Chalcedon

Cyzicus

PHRYGIA

P E R S I A N

E M P I R E

Hermus R.

Sardis

LYDIA

Maeander R.

Smyrna

Cyme

Phocaea

Clazomenae

Colophon

Ephesus

CARIA

Halicarnassus

Miletus

Cnidus

RHODES

CYNOS SEMA

COS

MYCALE

SAMOS

ERYTHRAE

IONIA

CHIOS

LESBOS

Mitylene

Assos

ARGINUSAE IS.

A E G E A N

S E A

CYCLADES

NAXOS

DELOS

PAROS

THERA

MELOS

CRETE

Gortyn

Carystus

EUBOEA

Chalcis

Eretria

Thebes

Delphi

AETOLIA

ACARNANIA

Naupactus

ACHAEA

Corinth

Megara

Athens

AEGINA

Methone

ARCADIA

Mantinea

Olympia

Elis

MESSENIA

Pylos

Argos

Sparta

CYTHERA

37

banned Megarians from the harbors and markets of the Aegean; later, at a meeting of Spartan allies at Sparta to discuss going to war, the Corinthians warned that the sea was vital, even for those who lived inland off the main trade routes.[14]

Although it was useful to suppress piracy and protect Athenian grain supplies, the main objective of thalassocracy was Athenian political and military mastery of the Aegean world. At its height Athens ruled directly 179 states which included perhaps 2,000,000 Greeks; the most remote of these were only an eight-day voyage (200–250 miles) from Athens. But Athenian naval power could be projected over the Mediterranean from Sicily to Egypt and the Black Sea, so that the world which had to consider Athenian policy seriously embraced perhaps 20,000,000 people.[15]

The fruits of Athenian naval mastery were many and varied. On the Acropolis rose the Parthenon, the most perfect and expensive Doric temple ever built, thanks to imperial revenues; beside it stood the Erechtheum and the Propylaea. Down below in the Agora appeared other religious and secular buildings; farther afield the hall of mysteries at Eleusis, the temple crowning the crags of Sunium, and other magnificent edifices were constructed as visible testimony to Athenian hegemony. In earlier days Athens had not been distinguished as a literary center. Now the tragic and comic stages came into existence; Herodotus spent some time at Athens, and by the end of the century Thucydides was writing his somber tale of the Peloponnesian War; then too Socrates was exploring the way a man should live. It would be too much to ascribe the birth of tragedy, comedy, and history to Athenian imperialism—Aeschylus, after all, was a mature man in 480 and fought in the battle of Salamis—but the vibrant, optimistic tone of Athenian life certainly helped to incite the support of the audiences attending the plays in the theater of Dionysus or the auditors of the Father of History.

Although most citizens continued to be land-rooted, the industrial and commercial sectors of Athens and its port of Piraeus became far more important. In the decades before 500 the city of Athens had numbered no more than about 10,000 inhabitants; by the close of the fifth century they had swelled probably to about 100,000, including "naval architects, shipbuilding contractors, merchants who now dealt exclusively in timber and pitch from the northern Aegean, cinnabar from Kea, hemp and flax, and leather" as well as tavernkeepers, ladies of the night, bands of cutthroats, and other fruits of naval power.[16] The port itself was restructured by Hippodamus of Miletus, the first urban planner to take into account economic as well as religious and political requirements; one comic poet could even proclaim, "Just as the Parthenon is beautiful so is the Piraeus."[17]

Athens had been fully democratic since the reforms of Cleisthenes, but across the fifth century the assembly of citizens became ever more the font of political power. Oddly enough, Thucydides, though discussing early Greek history almost exclusively as measured by the rise of interest in the sea, does not comment on the interconnection of imperialism abroad and democracy at home, but another writer known as the Old Oligarch saw these ties in his ironical comment:

> It is only just that the poorer classes and the common people of Athens should be better off than the men of birth and wealth, seeing that it is the people who man the fleet and have brought the city her power. The steerman, the boatswain, the lieutenant, the lookout-man at the prow, the shipwright—these are the people who supply the city with power rather than her heavy infantry and men of birth and quality.[18]

Pericles, the political leader from about 450, instituted pay for jurors, who were the older part of the population, and according to Plutarch initiated his building program partly to provide work for the poor.

Not everyone in Athens approved either of overseas imperialism or its internal political and social effects. The Old Oligarch rhetorically proclaimed that "in a country which bases its power on the navy . . . we become slaves of our slaves," and a foreigner, Stesimbrotus of Thasos, laid the responsibility on Themistocles who "degraded the people of Athens to the rowing pad and the oar."[19] In 445 Thucydides son of Melesias (not the historian) challenged Pericles in an ostracism as using imperial monies for the decoration of Athens, but himself lost; the citizen body as a whole followed Pericles, who later told the assembly that sea power implied tyranny but was justified by Athenian greatness. Loyalty to democracy then and later was always centered in the Piraeus.[20]

The most evident burden on the empire itself was the requirement of paying tribute to Athens. By 431 the voluntary contributions set half a century earlier had turned into forced payments. Very few states still had the option of furnishing ships, and by the Currency Decree of 449, which ordered the use of Athenian coinage, weights, and measures throughout the empire, the funds now came in the form of standardized Athenian tetradrachms, the "owls," struck in greater abundance than any previous Greek coinage.[21] These funds were safeguarded by Athena and like a good banker she took her fees by exacting one-sixtieth of each state's payment. These amounts were duly inscribed on stone slabs that fortunately have survived more or less intact and give us a detailed picture of imperial receipts.[22] The funds from the subjects also met the heavy expenses involved in maintaining a fleet that was at sea a great part of every year to keep the empire under control.[23]

Unlike the Roman Republic, which required from its Italian "allies" not cash but men for the Roman wars, the Athenian empire does not appear as a rule to have levied contingents of subjects for its galleys. There is one reference to impressment for the great expedition to Syracuse; otherwise considerable numbers of allies were tempted by pay to serve as mercenaries alongside the poorer Athenian citizens drafted for the rowers' benches;[24] Athens could never have manned its large fleets in the Peloponnesian War from its own citizen body. Daily pay rose across the fifth century from three obols to six, partly out of this necessity.

To supervise the empire, however, the Athenians made considerable use of garrisons and settled clumps of individual citizens called cleruchs on the lands of doubtful subjects; "residents" also served as standing checks, and traveling inspectors (episkopoi), whose arrogance was mocked by Aristophanes, toured the empire. The fourth-century work, Constitution of the Athenians, reckons these supervisors at 700 a year. In various decrees the independence of local courts was trimmed to require that capital penalties (death, exile, and loss of public rights) could be inflicted only by Athenian juries—as the Old Oligarch observed, this was good for the Athenian hotel business.[25]

These and similar measures, largely in place by 431, helped safeguard Athenian mastery, but they also directly violated the basic principle of Greek political life, *autonomia,* the right of a state to use its own laws.[26] Athens could accept any form of local government, including tyranny, but in the case of a revolt had no hesitation in imposing democracy on the rebels. In an ingenious article some years ago Ste. Croix sought to prove that the subjects generally were happy with Athenian rule inasmuch as it did protect local democracy, but a number of rebuttals have properly carried the day in opposition.[27] Stripped to its essence the Athenian empire produced "slavery" (*douleia*), and in the Peloponnesian War the Spartans were able to raise the battle cry of liberation from that enslavement by an Athenian elite. The true judgment of the subjects is evident in that whenever they saw a chance to escape from Athenian naval domination they revolted, and in 404 toppled the Athenian empire. It was most unfortunate that Athenian leaders could not know the pellucid and sagacious memorandum of Sir Eyre Crowe on the underlying responsibilities of naval powers if they were to keep their position:

> Sea power is more potent than land power, because it is as pervading as the element in which it moves and has its being. Its formidable character makes itself felt the more directly that a maritime State is, in the literal sense of the world, the neighbour of every country accessible by sea. It would, therefore, be but natural that the power of a State supreme at sea should inspire universal jealousy and fear, and be ever exposed to the danger of being overthrown by a general combination of the world. Against such a combination no single nation could in the long run stand, least of all a small island kingdom not possessed of the military strength of a people trained to arms, and dependent for its food on overseas commerce. The danger can in practice only be averted—and history shows that it has been so averted—on condition that the national policy of the insular and naval State is so directed as to harmonize with the general desires and ideals common to all mankind, and more particularly that it is closely identified with the

primary and vital interests of a majority, or as many as possible, of the other nations.[28]

In 431 Athens with its empire and Sparta with its allies came to open war, the famous Peloponnesian War immortalized by Thucydides, who decided at its outbreak that it was to be the greatest conflict ever in Greek history. For him the root cause was Spartan fear of the ever growing power of Athens, but though he tried to exculpate Pericles it is clear that the political leader of Athens did much to bring about the war at the time it broke out. For modern students of sea power this protracted conflict provides as valuable guidance as the vicissitudes of British naval history from the seventeenth to the twentieth century, both in understanding the utility of sea power and also in the dangers of overreliance on this one factor.

The first phase of the war from 431 to 421 was a contest of the elephant and the whale. The Peloponnesian league had only limited naval strength and did not possess the funds either to build a large navy or hire the necessary rowers. Although its powerful army invaded and laid waste Attica, it could not attack Athens proper, which was safe behind its stone walls and drew much of its food from overseas; nor were the Spartans able to keep their army active throughout the agricultural season. Sparta stood for liberty, but it could not aid Athenian subjects overseas to secure their freedom. When Mitylene rebelled in 428–27 the Athenian fleet inexorably reduced it once more to obedience.

On the other hand Athens could not force Sparta to surrender, for it dared not meet the invincible Spartan hoplites by land. Pericles had laid down the fundamental lines along which Athens would fight. When the enemy invaded Attica its citizenry abandoned their ancestral homes and poured into the safe refuge of the city until the Spartans retreated. Although they raged against Pericles and even temporarily removed him from office, he calmly adhered to his policy of wearing down the enemy by naval raids about the Peloponnesus. Above all, Athens must keep its fleet intact, on which rested its imperial revenues and its overseas supplies of grain. This cautious approach, very similar to the English naval strategy during the Napoleonic wars, could not bring victory, but it could avoid defeat.

Down to 421 the Athenians had the better of the widely scattered actions. Sparta itself they could not touch, but at points about the Peloponnesus they set up coastal forts to which disaffected helots and others might escape. Corinth, on the other hand, suffered severely. The Athenians secured naval mastery in the Gulf of Corinth through the brilliant battles of their admiral Phormio, and from their base of Naupactus they virtually prevented Corinthian trade to the west. By a chance of war the Athenian fleet cut off a whole battalion of Spartans on an island at Pylos and forced it to surrender. Among other prisoners were 120 Spartan "Equals," a sizable proportion of the Spartan citizen body, and the Spartans thereafter dared not invade Attica lest these hostages be executed.[29]

The last major actions in the first phase of the war took place along the coast of Macedonia, where a brilliant Spartan leader, Brasidas, was able to get at Athenian subject states by land and incite them to rebel. In a battle at Amphipolis both he and the radical Athenian leader Cleon were killed (422). Both sides were ready to call a halt to the inconclusive struggle, and the Spartans acquiesced in a peace treaty that led to massive discontent and defection of their allies, whose grounds of complaint against Athens were almost ignored in the treaty.

Athens had done as well, or better, than could have been expected. The Aegean empire was intact; in western waters its power had risen; the Peloponnesian league had been sorely shaken. Throughout history a naval power has usually been able to defeat a land power only if it secures a powerful land ally; but no major Greek state had been willing to link itself to Athenian imperialism. Argos, the one possibility, had been bound to neutrality by a treaty with Sparta that expired in 421.

Yet the Athenians were far from satisfied inasmuch as their eager expansionism had been essentially checked. During the strains of war the temperament of the assembly became steadily harsher, especially after Pericles died in 429, a victim of a great epidemic akin to typhus; the more vengeful rabble-rouser Cleon had then become its main adviser. The epidemic and overcrowding affected everyone; the devastation of the countryside and the losses of the army in several land battles damaged the rural classes especially.

Now that the war was over, Athenian opinions were sharply divided, and so was Athenian leadership. Nicias, a conservative aristocrat, was a second Pericles, except that his religious piety and high sense of duty were not matched by equal firmness and clarity of thought. Far more radical was the handsome and popular Alcibiades, a pupil of Socrates. First Alcibiades persuaded the Athenians to ally themselves with Argos and attempt land operations in the Peloponnesus; though the upshot was a defeat of the Argives and a small Athenian force at Mantinea (418), the peace was not formally broken.

Then came a tempting opportunity to intervene in the affairs of Sicily. During the war the Athenians had made some diplomatic and naval gestures toward unseating its main power, Syracuse; now an appeal from the native state of Segesta promised more extensive local support. Nicias stood in opposition and pointed out the basic strategic requirement that Athens remain powerful in the Aegean, but Alcibiades successfully rallied the spirit of excitement and possible economic profits among the citizens. The assembly not only voted to send an expedition but also set its size on the large scale that Nicias had proclaimed necessary; and it placed in command a triumvirate consisting of Nicias, Lamachus (a professional general), and Alcibiades. That in itself was almost enough to ensure disaster for the greatest amphibious operation ever launched in Greek history, but the fleet of some 100 triremes and troopships rowed out of the harbor of Piraeus in gala array (June 415), met a further contingent off Corcyra, and set course for Sicily.

The main Syracusan leader, Hermocrates, tried in vain to convince his fellow citizens to meet the Athenians on the sea;[30] but the Athenian leaders gave the Syracusans time to prepare by land as they fell to wrangling among themselves about the proper course of action. Alcibiades was soon recalled by his enemies in Athens on grounds that he had profaned the sacred Eleusinian mysteries during a drunken revel. Rather than return to face the probability of death, Alcibiades fled to Sparta where he urged the Spartans to aid Syracuse and to resume the war against Athens. Although Sparta sent only the general Gylippus to command the Corinthian relief expedition to Syracuse, this leader invigorated the Syracusans to withstand a great siege by the Athenian force.

Lodged in a swampy corner of the great harbor of Syracuse, Nicias grew more and more despondent and called for help, which was provided by a further expedition in 413. When the Athenians still failed to carry the city, their commanders decided to retreat by sea; but since an eclipse of the moon had just occurred, Nicias refused to leave for 27 days. During that period the Syracusans strengthened their ships and in a hand-to-hand naval battle in the great harbor defeated the Athenian forces. When finally Nicias led off his dejected army by land, they were cut to pieces by Syracusan cavalry. Nicias and the other Athenian leaders were executed, the Athenians died of hunger and thirst in the quarries where they were imprisoned, and the Athenian subjects were sold into slavery. All told 50,000 men and over 200 triremes were lost in one of the most poorly conceived amphibious operations ever attempted in history.

By 413 Sparta was again at war with Athens. Finances were so imperiled that Athens had to shift to a general tax of 5% on seaborne commerce; the Athenian empire tottered amid widespread disaffection and even revolt among its subjects. Spartan fleets could cruise the Aegean almost at will and were aided by contingents from Syracuse and other west Greek states, but the Athenians stubbornly held on, aided by Spartan indecisiveness— "the Spartans proved to be the most remarkably helpful enemies that the Athenians could have had."[31]

In the earlier stages of the war the Persian satraps of Asia Minor remained uncommitted, but from 411 on they came to the aid of Sparta by providing funds with which it could really challenge Athenian hegemony. Spartan admirals, unfortunately, lost battle after battle, but finally the able commander Lysander took charge and on September 1, 405, swooped across the Hellespont, where the Athenian fleet lay anchored at Aegospotami, and seized its ships while the crews were mostly on shore. He then swept down the Aegean, driving ahead of him all the Athenian colonists to Athens, which helplessly endured a siege by sea and land for several months before starvation forced surrender.

Athenian thalassocracy had failed but not entirely through its own inherent weaknesses. True, the Athenians could never get a useful land ally, as the British were generally able to do in their wars with France, Spain, and Germany; they also treated their dependent states as subjects while the Spartans presided over an alliance in which the allies had a real voice. The fundamental cause of defeat nonetheless was the ability of the Spartan political and military system to endure the stress of war and produce able commanders whereas Athenian democracy proved unstable and was led ever more poorly by demagogues. The Spartans also discovered that victory could be reached only by attaining naval mastery; they and the Romans later are almost unique in all history in facing the need to gain naval power and actually securing it.

After the surrender of Athens the allies of Sparta wished to see the oppressor city destroyed, but Sparta was content to tear down its Long Walls to the accompaniment of flute-girls, restrict its navy to 12 ships, and install an oligarchy. Sparta remained master of the Aegean world by land and by sea until it fell at odds with Persia over the Greek states of Asia Minor, which were to be surrendered to the Persians in repayment for their financial aid; when Sparta went back on its bargain the Persians reenforced the Phoenician fleet, hired the former Athenian admiral Conon, and in 394 defeated the Spartan navy in the battle of Cnidus. Thereafter Persia was the hidden master of Greek politics until the rise of Macedonia. When Athens ventured to interfere in Asia Minor during the reign of Artaxerxes he threatened to send his navy into the Aegean, and Athens evacuated Asia at once.

As this event may suggest, Athens had quickly recovered its democratic structure, its economic strength, and its cultural position; during the fourth century Athens was far more the center of the Greek world than it had ever been. It rebuilt its Long Walls, constructed a great arsenal at the naval port of Zea on the east side of the Piraeus promontory, and even had the financial

strength to fashion a new navy that had 120 active ships in 356
and 170 in 322 (its dockyards inventories eventually list no less
than 360 trireme hulls).[32] Although Athens dared not incur
Persian hostility it was at least master of the western Aegean
waters.

Why the new navy? Largely because it was useful in protecting
the route of supply from south Russia; Athenian warships went
as far as the Crimea to convoy grain ships and Athens' might was
exerted against such states as Byzantium when they sought to
interfere with the flow of grain. By law Athenian traders had to
bring grain to Athens, and only one-third could again be exported; "the foreign policy of the Athenians was largely a grain
policy."[33] Athenian commerce also needed protection against
pirates; several naval cruises were designed specifically to put
down these predators, and Athens even established a colony at
the head of the Adriatic to protect its merchants from Illyrian
marauders.[34] Trade had become ever more important to Athens;
an envoy could assert in its assembly, "The majority of you
derive your livelihood from the sea, or things connnected with
it. . . . The sea is your natural element—your birthright."[35]
Also important in nurturing naval interest was the memory of
Athenian greatness on the sea in the past; by the fourth century
orators and pamphleteers such as Demosthenes and Isocrates
often incorporated in their arsenal of arguments an appeal to the
pride of the Athenians in their earlier history.

Athenian public finances were always hand-to-mouth, and in
the fourth century were burdened by far greater charges to support the poorer citizens by payment for attending the assembly
and even the public festivals. Yet there were sufficient resources
to build and maintain the navy. For a time there was a second
Athenian confederacy, supported by the willingness of the island
states to aid in assuring peaceful seas, but the limited contributions of the league came to an end by 357, when Athens again
showed signs of imperialistic tendencies. Thereafter Athens had
to depend on its own income, tapped by means of a revision of
the system of trierarchs.[36]

In the fifth century each trireme had had a captain or trierarch, appointed for a year by the board of generals, who had not

only to command his vessel but to keep it in good order. Through the opening years of the Peloponnesian War this post was more a responsibility than a burden, and one citizen, Clinias, had even provided his own ship and crew in the Persian wars.[37] The stresses after 431 made the task so onerous that at times two wealthy men were appointed to share the position, as remained the custom in the fourth century. In 357 a panel of the 1200 richest citizens was organized, with subpanels or symmories to provide trierarchs and the funds for the running expenses of ships. Resident aliens could be appointed and even a man such as Isocrates could serve as trierarch when over 80 years of age, operating through a contractor.[38] About 340 Demosthenes carried out a further reorganization that limited the panel of possible trierarchs to the 300 wealthiest citizens.

Theoretically, a trierarch secured his warship at the beginning of the year from the 10 overseers of the dockyards, complete with tackle and sails; the oarsmen were drafted by the local units of government, the demes. Provision of food and so on was the responsibility of the generals. In practice, nonetheless, the system worked poorly. Apollodorus, a new citizen, was proud in 360 to be appointed trierarch but had largely to recruit his own rowers, provide better tackle, and pay his men for their food when the general failed to do so; moreover much of his crew deserted. "My men, knowing that they were skilled oarsmen, went off to take jobs wherever they figured they could get the highest pay."[39] It is a marvel that the navy remained a valuable asset to Athens.

Across the middle years of the fourth century Philip of Macedonia wove his way through the complicated tissue of Greek politics to become ever more powerful; in 338 his army met and defeated the citizens levies of Athens and Thebes at Chaeronea. Thebes he treated brutally; to Athens he was much more forgiving, partly because of its proud cultural inheritance but also because he needed the aid of its navy. When his son Alexander succeeded to the throne and carried out Philip's plan to invade Asia Minor, he actually made little use of Aegean naval resources, and instead carried out the most ingenious scheme of dealing with hostile sea power ever executed in history; he simply marched along the Levantine coast as far as Egypt, taking the

Persian ports as he went. The strategy required two major battles by land and the long-protracted siege of Tyre, the most famous in antiquity, but was in the end successful.

A recent eulogy of sea power asserts, "The sea has supplied mobility, capability and support throughout Western history, and those failing in the sea power test—notably Alexander, Napoleon and Hitler—also failed the longevity one."[40] Whatever may be the truth concerning Napoleon and Hitler, this is meaningless rhetoric as applied to Alexander. When he had reached the farthest end of his conquests in India he had a fleet constructed to operate in the Persian Gulf, and only the fact that neither he nor his admiral Nearchus was aware of the monsoon winds prevented his ships from providing food and water for the return march to Babylon across the Gedrosian desert. In preparation for his next adventure, the conquest of Arabia, he even had warships disassembled and transported overland from Phoenicia to Babylon.[41] It was Caesar, not Alexander, who several times came close to disaster by failing to make proper use of the sea.

After the death of Alexander in 323 his Macedonian regent Antipater faced a general revolt in Greece, which he put down without mercy. To counter the Athenian navy he summoned Phoenician forces which eliminated that fleet in the battle of Amorgos in 322. So ended almost two centuries of Athenian naval power, which had helped to protect and nourish one of the most remarkable cultural outbursts of all time. The future on the sea lay in the hands of the great monarchies carved out of Alexander's empire and also to a state that thus far had played no role in naval history.[42]

CHAPTER IV

The Age of Monster Fleets

When Alexander died in Babylon in 323 he had a posthumous son and a half-brother among other kin. Unfortunately he also left a group of extremely able marshals; in a few years all of Alexander's blood had been exterminated, their survival too threatening, as the generals fell to fighting for the inheritance of the vast empire. Temporarily the wily satrap of Phrygia, Antigonus the One-Eyed, gained control of everything save Macedonia and Egypt; the latter had been seized by Ptolemy immediately after Alexander's death, together with Cyprus, the south coast of Asia Minor, and several Aegean posts.[1]

Coping with Ptolemy would require a fleet, so Antigonus set to work to build his own navy, but on that large scale which characterized all his schemes. Eight thousand men were employed in cutting timber from the Lebanon and Taurus mountains, and shipbuilding centers were created at Tripolis, Byblos, Sidon and also in Cilicia; even Rhodes accepted a part in the naval preparations though it tended to favor Ptolemy. His son Demetrius was assigned naval responsibility and in 306 justified his appointment by destroying the Ptolemaic fleet off Salamis in Cyprus; Ptolemy lost 120 warships, 180 transports, and most of his overseas empire.[2] Demetrius went on in 305 to attack Rhodes by land and sea but failed in one of the most famous sieges in antiquity. Then the other generals combined against Antigonus and in 301 defeated and killed him in the battle of Ipsus. Demetrius survived and held power for a time in the Aegean but dissipated his strength and died a captive.

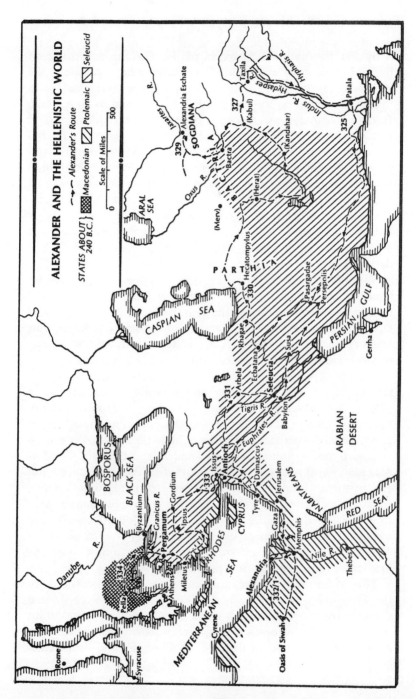

ALEXANDER AND THE HELLENISTIC WORLD

STATES ABOUT 240 B.C.
- - - → Alexander's Route
▦ Macedonian ▨ Ptolemaic ▨ Seleucid

Scale of Miles
0   500

Rome

Danube R.

BOSPORUS
BLACK SEA
Byzantium
Granicus R.
Pella ×334
Gordium
Ipsus
Pergamum
Athens
Miletus
RHODES
CYPRUS
SEA
Syracuse
MEDITERRANEAN SEA
Cyrene
Issus
×333
Antioch
Tyre
Damascus
Jerusalem
Gaza
Alexandria
×332/1
Memphis
NABATAEANS
RED SEA
Thebes
Nile R.
Oasis of Siwah

ARABIAN DESERT

Euphrates R.
Tigris R.
Babylon
Seleucia
Susa
Ecbatana
Arbela
×331
Rhagae
Hecatompylus
×330
PARTHIA
(Merv)
(Herat)
BACTRIA
Bactra
SOGDIANA
×329
Alexandria Eschate
Jaxartes R.
Oxus R.
ARAL SEA
CASPIAN SEA

Pasargadae
Persepolis
PERSIAN GULF
Gerrha

(Kabul)
×327
(Kandahar)
Taxila
Indus R.
Hydaspes R.
Hyphasis R.
×325
Patala

By 301 the political structure of the Hellenistic world was beginning to take shape in three prominent dynasties: the Ptolemaic in Egypt; the Seleucid in Asia Minor, Syria, and on to the borders of India; and eventually the Antigonid in Macedonia. In the latter there was some sense of what may be called national loyalty; in the others Macedonian and Greek generals and bureaucrats controlled native populations for their own profit and power. The interstate relations of this era were as complicated in dynastic marriages and feuds as were those of early modern Europe and produced a great deal of hostilities by land and sea. Since the present study is not a general history we may pass lightly over specific wars; the manner in which sea power was used in practice led to a very unexpected result, that is, the destruction of the Hellenistic state system.

Not only were the political units much larger than the earlier Greek *poleis,* so too were the squadrons launched in Mediterranean naval warfare across the centuries to the final victory of Octavian in 31 B.C.; also the warships of the age were behemoths when compared to triremes. Early in the fourth century Dionysius of Syracuse had introduced ships called in Latin quadriremes and quinqueremes which evidently had sets of four and five rowers respectively. The usual interpretation is that instead of tugging individual oars as in the trireme larger groups manipulated great sweeps, the Venetian system *a scaloccio,* though in an alternative explanation quadriremes had two banks of two oarsmen each and a quinquereme two and three.[3] Before the end of Athenian naval strength it too was building the larger ships, and Hellenistic navies came to be composed largely of quinqueremes, with crews of some 300 rowers, which were almost impregnable to attacks by the smaller old-style galleys.[4] Indeed numbers of oarsmen crept up as far as 10 and 16; Ptolemy II even boasted a 40, which was probably a catamaran in construction, with groups of 20 rowers on each side, in a parade vessel.

This change was the consequence of two other alterations. In the first place crews especially of Egyptian ships were drafted from the countryside and had no naval training; more important perhaps was the revolution in tactics, which much reduced the reliance on maneuver, exhibited by Phormio and other commanders in the great days of Athenian thalassocracy. Warships now were fully decked and equipped with stone- and arrow-throwing machines and much larger complements of marines. It would not be exactly true to say, as one modern student does, that Hellenistic admirals "were content to see naval actions as opportunities for men in full armour to fight it out on deck,"[5] for in the rather chaotic seafight off Chios in 201 there was a great deal of ramming and other maneuvers; but the statement can be applied, as we will see shortly, very aptly to Roman naval practice.

In the Hellenistic age economic interests played a more visible role in state policy. If there were six Syrian wars between the Ptolemies and Seleucids the causes were in part personal pride and desire for glory, but also the advantage to be gained from controlling the Mediterranean ports to which the luxuries of India and Arabia largely flowed. These wars did not involve any important naval combat, but another aspect of Ptolemaic objectives did do so.

The Ptolemaic system of exploitation of Egypt was designed to secure large supplies of wheat that could be sold abroad mainly through Rhodes as entrepot to provide funds for its foreign policy in the eastern Mediterranean, which was aimed at naval control of the Aegean.[6] This led directly to competition with Macedonia, firmly in the hands of Antigonus Gonatas, son of Demetrius, from 276 on. Athens and Sparta, spurred by Egyptian funds, launched the Chremonidean war against him probably in 267–63, but the Egyptian navy, though occupying some forts on the mainland, did nothing of any value; as its admiral Patroclus pointed out, his marines were only native Egyptians.[7] Subsequent naval conflict between Macedonia and Egypt is very poorly illuminated in our fragmentary sources "which continually tempt one to go off on a tangent."[8] There were at least two battles, off Cos about 255 and Andros in 245, both of which Macedonia won. Thereafter Ptolemaic attention to the Aegean waned. The uncertainties of these wars are well illustrated by the great statue on a staircase in the Louvre, the Victory of Samothrace, which depicts a figure of victory on the prow of a galley; often connected to Cos or Andros it most recently has been identified as a Rhodian dedication in the first decades of the second century, and not Macedonian at all.[9]

In general, "No Power maintained a standing fleet, that is, one always in commission, with one possible exception [Egypt]. . . . What is called the command of the sea, at this time, only meant that the Power who claimed it had a good prospect, if challenged, of getting a fleet to sea which might defeat the challenger."[10]

It was the island state of Rhodes, indeed, that played the most useful role in the eastern Mediterranean well into the second century. It had a squadron of about 30 quinqueremes, which were manned by citizens and commanded by essentially professional captains and admirals; Rhodian dockyards were so carefully guarded that one effort by a Macedonian king to set them afire badly miscarried. The state took seriously its responsibility of keeping the sea open for commerce and faced down one threat by Byzantium to levy tolls on Hellespontine traffic; it also did much to repress piracy, an effort for which one Rhodian admiral was publicly honored at Delos.[11] This policy was clearly appreciated by other states; following the devastating earthquake at Rhodes in 226 all the Hellenistic monarchs contributed timber and grain to restore and supply its ships, and Seleucus III even presented 10 quinqueremes already built and fully equipped.[12]

Hellenistic naval history, as we have seen, can scarcely be written and does not provide very useful illumination of the value of sea power except in the case of Rhodes. In any event, strength at sea in the eastern Mediterranean was to be coldly and swiftly eliminated by the intervention of a new naval power from the west.

Carthaginian mastery in this area had been unquestioned until the third century. Syracuse had supported a fleet large enough to defeat the Etruscans off Cumae in 474, but it never ventured seriously to oppose on the sea Carthaginian invasions of Sicily from 480 onwards; instead Dionysius used his new quadriremes and quinqueremes to secure control only of southern Italy and the Adriatic. In 264, however, a minor problem arising from the occupation of Messana by a band of mercenaries called Mamertines threw Carthage and Rome at odds.

The immediate occasion was an attack by Syracuse on the

Mamertines, who in desperation appealed both to Carthage and Rome for assistance. Carthage responded at once with men and ships; the Roman Senate, which normally made decisions in foreign policy, found itself in a quandary. If it intervened, it would face the Carthaginian supremacy on the sea; yet if it did nothing, Carthage would have a firm grasp on the vital strait between Sicily and Italy. Modern historians normally suggest that Rome was concerned in this respect purely for the sake of its south Italian Greek subjects, but in fact Roman trade by sea was far more vital than it is usually portrayed. By the early third century Rome was among the bigger cities of the Mediterranean, with a population of possibly some 90,000, and so large a mass of inhabitants required grain not only coming down the Tiber from Etruria but also by sea from Sicily and elsewhere. Since the Roman state at this time did not yet enjoy the profits of empire this grain had to be paid for, and there is adequate evidence that Roman potters, smiths, and other craftsmen made products that could be sold abroad. So too Roman ships plied Mediterranean waters; it was a Roman vessel that saved the Greek politician Aratus in a storm in the Adriatic in 254. The conventional picture of simple Roman tillers of the soil, created by Livy, Cicero, and other patriots of the Late Republic, is in reality very misleading.[13]

Yet what answer to give the Mamertines? The Senate finally referred the problem to the assembly of citizens, which voted to provide assistance, and so Roman military forces were despatched to south Italy, where they succeeded in crossing the strait and wresting control of Messana from the Carthaginians. The result was the First Punic War, which was to drag on from 264 to 241.[14]

Since Carthage did not have a nearby base from which it could successfully blockade the strait, Roman armies were free to enter Sicily and by 261 had conquered almost all the island save for the western stronghold of Lilybaeum. Then it became apparent that Rome could win total control only by gaining command of the sea from Carthage; the Senate, clear-headed on strategic matters, without hesitation proceeded to order the building of 20 triremes and 100 quinqueremes. Italy fortunately supported great forests of fir, preferred for warships, which could easily provide the necessary timber. Some ingenious shipwright, perhaps Greek, also devised a counter to Carthaginian superiority in naval tactics by equipping the Roman quinquereme with the "crow," a gang-plank fixed to the prow but capable of being pivoted and coming down with an iron spike on the deck of an enemy ship so that Roman soldiers could more easily pour over and turn the action into hand-to-hand conflict.[15]

In 260 the new Roman fleet rowed west along the north coast of Sicily and won a signal victory at Mylae over the enemy, whose ships were caught and fixed one by one; an elogium in the Roman Forum proudly but erroneously praised the admiral C. Duilius as the first Roman to venture on the sea.[16] Rather than besieging Lilybaeum, the Romans, once again focusing on the main problem, invaded Africa in 256 so as to strike directly at Carthage. To do so they had to meet the Carthaginian navy off Ecnomus, on the south shore of Sicily. The Roman ships were encumbered by the transport vessels for the army and arranged themselves in three lines as customary in their land battles. The two consuls Manlius and Regulus were in the van before the line of galleys towing the transports; a third line was in the rear. The Carthaginian admirals Hamilcar and Hanno weakened their center to draw the consuls on, and then their flank squadrons swooped around the sides to fall on the Roman rear. The end result, however, was not what the enemy had expected; the in-dividual Roman squadrons turned to meet the encircling threat, drove off the seaward ships in disarray, and penned the inshore Carthaginian ships against the coast. The Romans took 50 vessels and sank 30 others against a loss of only 24 Roman galleys. The consuls could then proceed to Africa and landed their army in Tunisia, but winter came before the Romans could launch a full attack on Carthage, heavily fortified. In despair, the Carthagin-ians turned to a Spartan mercenary general, Xanthippus, skilled in Hellenistic tactics, who combined Carthaginian infantry, Numidian cavalry, and elephants to defeat the Romans. The Roman navy evacuated the survivors; but its admirals disre-garded the warnings from their naval experts, and a storm off the south coast of Sicily destroyed almost all the fleet.

Thereafter Roman consuls squandered most of the replacements in 253 by insisting on sailing in heavy weather despite the advice of their pilots; as Polybius observed, "The Romans, to speak generally, rely on force in all their enterprises . . . when they come to encounter the sea and the atmosphere and choose to fight them by force they meet with signal defeats."[17] Between battles and storms about 600 Roman warships and 1000 transports were sunk; probably no naval war in history has seen such casualties by drowning.

After the Romans gave up the topheavy crow, a battle in 249 in which Claudius Pulcher foolishly pursued a Carthaginian squadron into the narrow harbor of Drepanum (on the west coast of Sicily) was a disaster, though that perhaps owed as much to the anger of the gods of Rome as to Carthaginian naval skill. Roman commanders always had to gain divine blessings before a battle; since it was impracticable to carry sacrificial cattle on shipboard, crates of sacred chickens were provided. From the way they pecked at grain soothsayers could divine the will of the gods, but on this occasion the chickens refused to do their duty. Claudius Pulcher, angered at their failure to cooperate, threw the crate into the sea with the observation that if they would not eat they could drink. The result was inevitable; nearly 100 warships were lost—the only serious defeat the Romans suffered by sea during the First Punic War.

For a time both Rome and Carthage lay in exhaustion, but finally the Senate assessed itself for funds to build a last flotilla of 200 warships. This expedition instituted a tighter watch at Lilybaeum; when the Carthaginians sent their galleys to break the blockade—but without a normal complement of marines, which was to be picked up at Lilybaeum—the Roman commander C. Lutatius Catulus took his stripped-down ships out despite stormy seas and crushed the relief fleet in the battle of the Aegates islands. Carthage had to sue for peace and yielded Sicily and naval mastery of the western Mediterranean to Rome. Almost immediately, the victor seized Sardinia and Corsica and thereafter used its navy to repress the piratical states on the Illyrian coast of the Adriatic.

The Romans kept a wary eye on Carthage, which rebuilt its strength in Spain. When the young, brilliant Hannibal became its general there from 221 on, the Romans were even more alarmed and finally sent ambassadors to Carthage to require his surrender. On its refusal, the Second Punic War began in 218, and the Romans prepared to launch a two-prong attack, one army being sent by sea to Spain to contain Hannibal, the other marching to Sicily to be ferried to Carthage. Their navy, which numbered 220 quinqueremes, was master of the sea as against only a few more than 50 Carthaginian vessels.[18]

The Romans, however, proceeded too slowly and failed to measure the audacity of Hannibal, who planned to invade Italy itself, overcome the Roman armies, and incite the subjects into rebellion. To do so he had to make his way from Spain to northern Italy, where the recently conquered Gauls could provide a base; contrary to the views of Mommsen and Mahan noted in the Introduction, he had to march by land not simply because the Romans controlled the sea but by reason of his large forces of cavalry and elephants that could not easily have been transported by sea. In one trap after another Hannibal decimated Roman armies, but he could never succeed in his essential aim; some Roman allies did revolt, but most remained loyal. From time to time Carthage could muster fleets but not large enough to meet Roman naval power or to reenforce Hannibal, who finally in a truce evacuated Italy. At the final battle in North Africa at Zama in 202 the Roman commander Scipio Africanus had the advantage in cavalry, for the Numidians had joined him, and, using Hannibalic tactics against Hannibal, won.

The peace of 201 was harsh—a "Carthaginian peace" in Keynes' famous term. Carthage yielded its elephants and all but 10 of its warships, surrendered Spain, and promised to pay a large indemnity. In the further agreement not to wage war in Africa itself without Roman approval lay seeds for later troubles that were eventually to bring the total destruction of Carthage (Third Punic War, 149–46). Rome itself was drained financially—and proceeded at once to intervene in the eastern Mediterranean.

This peculiar juxtaposition presents one of the most puzzling problems in Roman history. For the past two generations the conventional explanation has been that wily ambassadors from Rhodes and Pergamum, alarmed by the machinations of the

Seleucid king Antiochus III and Philip V of Macedonia, deftly played on Roman fears of Eastern despots and the philhellene enthusiasm of Roman aristocrats, now much more imbued with Greek culture, and so led Rome to declare war on Philip to "liberate" Greece. This, however, will not do; as a recent student has rightly commented, "the very idea of philhellenism as national policy would be unintelligible to a Roman."[19] Rome already had no reason to love Philip, who had declared war on it in 213 in concert with Hannibal so as to regain his claim to the Illyrian coast (First Macedonian War). He had been totally unable to face Roman naval strength and had concluded peace in 205, but Rome continued to show interest in Greek affairs.

Another powerful line of explanation, as noted earlier, has argued that Rome was deliberately imperialistic from the late fourth century onward to provide military reputations to its aristocrats as well as financial profit.[20] Despite support from some remarks of Polybius, the second-century historian who sought to account for the rise of Rome, this view also must be carefully qualified. Empires may not be created in a fit of absent-mindedness, but their evolution over many decades, even centuries, is not a result of conscious plans; as Harris himself puts it, one does not have to aim at empire to acquire one.

In the Second Macedonian War the Romans initially underestimated the support the Macedonians gave to their king and only after several stumbles reenforced their army sufficiently to defeat the Macedonian phalanx; in the peace treaty Philip surrendered almost all his navy. The war inevitably led to conflict with Antiochus III, who tried to regain ancestral territories in Asia Minor and Thrace. This time the Romans viewed the great Eastern conqueror with alarm and prepared both army and navy for serious action. Since their most experienced general Scipio Africanus now held a religious position that prevented him from commanding troops, his brother was made technical commander with Africanus as his "advisor." To counter the sizable Seleucid navy the Romans enlisted the aid of the Rhodians and mastered the enemy in the battle of Myonnesus: Antiochus was defeated on land, and in the ensuing peace of 189 he gave up all but 12 warships.[21] Since Egypt by this point was a broken reed, which was to need Roman aid several times in subsequent years, every naval power in the Mediterranean had vanished, save for Rome itself. Rhodes remained, but its turn soon came. When the son of Philip V, Perseus, led a Macedonian revolt against Roman overlordship (Third Macedonian War, 171–67), the Romans took the matter so lightly that their forces did not do well at the beginning; Rhodes made the serious blunder of sending envoys to Rome to mediate the conflict, but alas they arrived after the news of the final Roman success. The Senate saw no need for direct action; instead it struck at the heart of Rhodian strength by making the island of Delos a free port.[22] Thereafter Rhodes did not have the financial power to keep up its navy, though it continued to have some warships down to 42 B.C.

Rome had won its mastery of the eastern Mediterranean primarily by land battles, but wherever and whenever naval forces were useful they had been provided out of Roman resources of funds and men. The Romans gained control of the seas not through tactical skills; for Polybius the Carthaginians were superior in efficiency and equipment, but Rome was successful "owing to the gallantry of their men."[23] There were other factors as well.

Rome thus had the financial strength and the timber to build fleets that were always larger than those of their opponents; "history might have run a very different course if Italy had not been well forested."[24] To secure technical guidance it could draw on the skills of the Greeks in south Italian ports, who provided pilots and trainers of crews; in the initial Roman fleet of the First Punic War the crews were prepared by rowing in mock-ups on land. Rome also had the manpower to staff its navies just as it could raise legion after legion in the disasters of the war against Hannibal; and sailors as well as soldiers were generally loyal, though mutinies in Roman armies were not unknown. The admirals who directed the fleets were not brilliant, but dogged in carrying out their orders. The battle of Ecnomus was, in particular, a remarkable illustration of the ability of Roman consuls to keep control of their forces even when committed in battle, for their squadrons shifted positions to meet unexpected Carthaginian tactics enough to win the day.[25] Finally, the motive force for

Roman policy, the Senate, rarely failed to see what needed to be done and to execute its plans without hesitation.

A student of Latin poetry has carefully analyzed the view of the sea expressed therein and concludes that Roman poets at the most preferred to stand on the shore and simply look out at this hostile element. "What joy it is," said Lucretius, "when out at sea the storm winds are lashing the waters, to gaze from the shore at the heavy stress some other man is enduring!"[26] The Romans disliked the sea, but so too the early Greeks were equally distrustful of open waters; the enthusiasm of Athenian thalassocrats was not necessarily the norm, and true celebration of the challenge of the sea was to come only in modern Portuguese, Dutch, and English poetry. Yet when it became necessary for the Romans to provide fleets and utilize them for the ends of Roman policy they simply did so.

For the rest of ancient history power lay in the hands of Rome, "master of land and sea" as the Alexandrian poet Lycophron baldly put it.[27] During the last two centuries B.C., however, those hands were unsteady, often even palsied. This uncertainty critically tested the fundamental strengths of classical civilization and its economic structure as well as the system of government of the Roman Republic, which tottered ever more precariously. The Romans did not question their right to mastery; Cicero proudly proclaimed, "We have overcome all the nations of the world because we have realized that the world is directed and governed by the will of the gods."[28] But they proved not very eager to accept the concomitant burdens; as a result their rule came to be hated in much of the Greek East, where an intense debate raged on the problem whether Roman imperialism was justified or was the evil consequence of Chance (Tyche).[29]

Nowhere was this instability more critical than on the sea in the late second and early first centuries. The Romans had carried out the most complete process of naval disarmament that the world has ever seen and let their own naval establishment rot away. This cavalier dismissal of sea power produced retribution in one of the worst waves of piracy in classical times. Pirates could not base themselves on shores the Romans directly occupied, but there were other holes, partly in Crete but more handily in the rocky harbors of Cilicia.[30] The Romans made Cilicia a province in 102 to counter this threat, but their writ ran only in the lower, more open reaches of the eastern part of the area; Rocky Cilicia remained outside their control, and it must be admitted that the Romans were too eager to buy the slaves whom the pirates poured into the markets of Delos to be overly concerned at their depredations, at least at the outset.[31] According to one source, pirate vessels numbered a total of 1000, and 400 coastal settlements were sacked.

In 88 the Aegean erupted in a revolt against Roman misgovernment, which was led by the astute king of Pontus, Mithridates, who gained the adhesion even of the sleepy university town of Athens. He had his own fleet but was much assisted by the pirates; to counter his threat the Roman commander sent to the east, Sulla, had to recruit ships of his own from every available source. This makeshift force proved victorious and was the nucleus for a Roman naval revival in following decades; unlike the Punic wars, when the Roman navy was built by public funds, the Romans for some time relied only on requisitions from maritime cities, which were thus ordered in 84–83 to construct and lay up in reserve a number of ships for possible future use.[32]

This strength, ranging up to 100 vessels, was enough to cope with Mithridates when war broke out again, but it was far from adequate to master the pirates who tyrannized the East and extended their raids to the shores of Italy during the years 70–68. They seized two praetors for ransom, sank a Roman squadron in the port of Caieta, and seriously threatened the food supplies of the Roman masses. Rhetorically indicting Roman sloth, Cicero asserted, "Who sailed the seas without opening himself to the risk either of death or of slavery? . . . What province did you keep free from the pirates during these years? What source of revenue was secure for you? . . . How many islands do you suppose were deserted, how many of your allies' cities either abandoned through fear or captured by the pirates?"[33]

When the flow of grain to Rome was endangered, the city eventually reacted, and the popular hero Pompey was entrusted in 67 with powers over all the Mediterranean, the first extraordinary command in a chain that was to lead to the end of the Republic. Pompey divided the sea into 25 districts, each with its own ships and admirals, and in three months swept from the western end to Cilicia, eliminating the pirates without open engagement, and seized their native strongholds. Those who had become pirates "not through wickedness, but from poverty" he settled inland.[34] Sporadic piracy by sea was to continue for a few more decades, but essentially the Romans had learned the consequences of naval disarmament; as the terms of Pompey's triumph ran he "had restored the rule of the sea to the Roman people."[35]

In 58 Caesar began his own extraordinary command, this time in Gaul, which he conquered in the next few years. At home conservative senators feared ever more his growing power and engineered a break between Caesar and Pompey which led in 49–48 to the first great civil war of the dying Republic. Caesar invaded Italy so swiftly that Pompey and his senators had to flee to Greece, but Caesar was temporarily prevented from following him inasmuch as Pompey still held the navy under his control. Caesar ordered ships to be built in every Italian port; Pompey prepared his forces to return to Italy. As Cicero wrote to a friend, Pompey "holds with Themistocles that those who are masters of the sea will be victors in the end."[36]

Unfortunately the sea itself had its own ideas. When some ships were ready Caesar evaded the blockade of Brundisium and crossed the Adriatic in the winter of 48. The opposing admiral, Bibulus, caught some vessels on the return and sank them, but eventually Antony was able to bring over the rest of Caesar's army; the inability of galleys to catch sailing ships in a good wind has been noted in an earlier chapter. Although Pompey used his naval power to provide his own army and deny food to Caesar, the battlefield of Pharsalus in September 48 saw a complete Caesarian victory. Pompey fled to Egypt, where he was at once beheaded by the fearful Egyptian government; Caesar followed with far too few ships and men and was besieged for almost a year in the Ptolemaic palace at Alexandria—together with Cleopatra, sister of the king. Once land troops from Syria had

broken the siege Caesar returned briefly to Rome, but then once
again with inadequate naval strength invaded Africa to end Pompeian resistance there. On land Caesar was a tactical genius, who
inspired the blind loyalty of his troops; but on the sea he was
barely competent—even in invading Britain during his Gallic
campaign he failed to realize that there were tides in the Atlantic
and so had his ships stranded on the coast.

After his murder on the Ides of March 44 Antony took command at the outset but soon faced the challenge of the Younger
Caesar, a grandnephew only 18 years of age, who had been
adopted in Caesar's will as his son. Octavian, as he was called
for a few years, was determined to avenge the murder of his "father." First he secured an army of his own, largely from Caesar's
veterans, and forced his election as consul in 43. Then he joined
with Antony and a secondary leader, Lepidus, to form a cabal
(the Second Triumvirate) that avenged itself on opponents and
also raised funds by proscribing many Roman leaders, including
Cicero. Finally, Antony and Octavian marched east and destroyed
the tyrannicides Brutus and Cassius at Philippi in Macedonia.
Thereafter Antony took the east (and Cleopatra) and Octavian
the west, which involved settling a large number of veterans on
confiscated lands.

To add to his unpopularity Octavian faced a serious threat in
the son of the great Pompey, Sextus Pompey, who had gained
most of his navy and used it from bases in Sicily and Sardinia to
master the Tyrrhenian and put pressure on Rome by interfering
with its grain supply. Slaves, the proscribed, and other discontented elements ran off to join Sextus, but Octavian initially had
no naval strength to meet this threat.

A temporary peace was arranged between the two by Antony
in 39, but open warfare broke out the next year. Sextus' pressure
on Roman food supplies became even more dangerous, and
Octavian was almost mobbed in the Forum on one occasion by
hungry citizens. He built fleets at Rome and Ravenna and began
a dextrous campaign of propaganda, at which he was becoming a
master, to portray Sextus as a glorified brigand; either by force
or voluntarily, the wealthy of Italy, irked by Sextus' reception

of runaway slaves and angered by his plundering, supported Octavian by furnishing money and rowers. The problem of manning a fleet in the western Mediterranean, moreover, was now easier, for the civil wars had scattered seafarers over all the coasts.

Yet Octavian's first squadrons were destroyed in storms and defeat. Determined to cope with Sextus, he recalled his main military aide Agrippa from Gaul to build new warships in 37. A flotilla was constructed near Naples in an artificial harbor, and the new ships were built far more heavily than those of Sextus; to secure rowers Octavian took the unusual step of recruiting 20,000 slaves, but he freed them before formal enlistment.[37] Finally in 36 Agrippa won decisively off Sicily, though Octavian himself had at one point to flee to Italian shores. Sextus escaped, but soon was executed by one of Antony's governors. A gilded statue of Octavian was erected in the Forum bearing the inscription "Peace, long disturbed, he re-established on land and sea."[38] Roman leaders of the previous generation had been rudely educated by the pirate scourge as to the importance of keeping firm hands on the sea; Octavian himself learned by bitter experience the same lesson.

Soon Antony, bewitched according to Virgil by the Oriental siren Cleopatra, was drawn into war with Octavian. The fact that the struggle was settled by naval battle reflects the importance sea power had attained, but the final result was clearly foreshadowed by the physical and psychological skirmishing before the battle proper. Antony and Cleopatra came up to Greece in the winter of 32–31, where many of their rowers died of a plague. Agrippa in the spring of 31 quickly snatched the initiative by bold attacks on Antony's supply lines to Egypt, and through one of the most skillful campaigns of ancient times hemmed in Antony by the summer on the west coast of the Balkans. On September 2 Antony sought to break out from the Gulf of Actium, but his disaffected navy with its poorly trained rowers fought badly. Cleopatra fled, and Antony deserted the struggle to follow her to Egypt.

After asserting his authority in Greece Octavian also made his way to Egypt with overwhelming forces by land and sea. Antony and Cleopatra committed suicide; on August 1, 31 B.C., the victor entered Alexandria, where he looked down on the embalmed body of Alexander. The great Macedonian had begun as unquestioned king; Octavian had commenced his career as a virtual school boy two years younger and now was master of the Mediterranean world.

CHAPTER V

The Roman Imperial Peace

Alexander died at the age of 33; on his final victory Octavian—or as he was soon to be named Imperator Caesar Augustus divi filius—had another 45 years in which to consolidate a superb system of veiled but complete mastery and pass it on to succeeding emperors of the Roman world. Deftly he inured the ostentatious, militaristic senatorial class to support his position; by care for the food, water, and entertainment of the Roman masses he gained their loyalty; provision of more orderly government and protection of justice in the provinces led to his acceptance by the upper classes of the cities in an unwritten bargain to trade imperial fealty for local control.

To safeguard his own authority and also the world he ruled Augustus devoted careful attention to a great military reorganization in which he probably was aided by Agrippa.[1] The solution was to create a professional, long-term army. Its backbone consisted of citizens, theoretically at least volunteers, who were organized in heavy infantry divisions, the legions, some of which were to last 400 years—the longest-lived units in history. Alongside the legions served non-citizens, provincials who were recruited initially from tribal units in smaller auxiliary groups of infantry or cavalry. Together, the army of legions and auxilia numbered about 250,000 men, but it had to garrison some 4000 miles of frontiers in Europe, Asia, and Africa as well as maintaining internal order. The expense of this force was the main obligation of the state budget, but the prosperity of the Roman Empire in the first two centuries after Christ was able to bear this burden.

Augustus also proceeded to the parallel, systematic creation of a permanent navy. After Actium he had 400 vessels of his own to which he now could add roughly 300 of Antony's ships. Ten of these, including Antony's flagship, were dedicated to Actian Apollo; others were burned or scrapped as surplus; the remainder were sent to Forum Iulii on the south coast of Gaul, which had been used as a naval base against Sextus Pompey. With this event the history of the Roman imperial navy formally begins; thereafter the Empire had standing naval forces almost as long as it was an effective state.[2] As Tacitus commented on the Augustan system, "the empire's frontiers were on the ocean or distant rivers. Armies, provinces, fleets, the whole system was interrelated."[3] The role of the navy was well put by a scholar years ago, "We hear very much about the influence of Roman roads in promoting Roman civilization, but the influence of Roman fleets in bringing about that miracle has been almost entirely ignored. Yet it is demonstrable that the Roman empire depended quite as much on its fleets as on its roads."[4]

Although Forum Iulii continued to be a base for several decades, it was essentially supplanted by two great war harbors in Italy itself. One was Misenum, just north of Naples, near the ports of western Italy, as close to Rome as any other good harbor in Italy at the time; moles guarded an inner and outer harbor and a reservoir of Augustan date husbanded its water supplies. The other base was artificially constructed on a lagoon south of Ravenna, connected by a canal to the Po River. Subsidiary detachments from these two Italian flotillas, of temporary or permanent character, are attested by tombstones of sailors and literary references.[5]

To judge from the number of surviving tombstones and names of ships, the *classis Misenensis* was larger than the *classis Ravennas* and had the imperial flagship, but both were large enough to provide a whole legion in the civil wars of A.D. 68–69 (and the Misene fleet another temporary legion). If it appears odd that sailors could thus be turned into soldiers, it must be remembered that the crew of each galley was organized not only on naval lines but also as a military century under a centurion; sailors had themselves depicted on tombstones in military dress and called themselves *milites*, not *nautae*.[6] The strength of the two squadrons may be estimated at some 15,000 men; provincial flotillas in the Mediterranean and on the northern rivers were perhaps in total as strong so that the Roman imperial navy, as we may call a structure never unified under one command, totalled about 30,000 men.

The largest units were based on Italy partly for geographical reasons, inasmuch as the peninsula was the center of the Mediterranean Sea, and at this time the primary trade routes tended to run to Italian ports. Also Italy traditionally was exempt from military garrisons, but the presence of the navy could be tolerated and gave the emperors direct, sure control both of Italy and of avenues of approach.[7] The fact, however, that command was divided reflects Augustus' caution in keeping his generals, and admirals, from gaining too independent a position. The prefects of the fleets were not even senators, as was true of legionary commanders (save in Egypt), but came from the second rung of the Roman aristocracy, the equestrians, who could not easily attempt rebellion; in the early decades, indeed, some prefects were even freedmen, and equestrian prefects themselves were low on the ranks of the military hierarchy. Only once were both fleets placed under a single commander, though they cooperated in policing the Mediterranean. The most famous prefect of the Misene fleet was Pliny the Elder, the polymath author of the *Natural History* and several historical works, who died from exploring too closely the fumes of the eruption of Mt. Vesuvius in 79; three other naval prefects, however, reached the highest military post in the Empire, that of praetorian prefect.

The sailors themselves were certainly not citizens, unlike the legionaries, but they were not slaves as Mommsen and others asserted on flimsy evidence; rather they were provincials, largely from the Balkans and Egypt, who volunteered to serve for 26 years (28 by the third century).[8] Letters preserved in Egyptian papyri reflect their enthusiasm on enlistment, such as that of Apion to his father, hoping for speedy promotion: "I send you a little picture of myself by Euktemon. My name is now Antonius Maximus."[9] As the last remark suggests, sailors were subject to the process of Romanization, including the use of Latin. From

ATLANTIC OCEAN

BRITAIN

GERMANS

Elbe R.

Rhine R.

MARCOMANNI

QUADI

GAUL

Alesia

Danube

RAETIA

NORICUM

Lugdunum

Rhone R.

CISALPINE
GAUL

PANNONIA

NARBONENSIS

Massilia

Ravenna

DALMATIA

FARTHER SPAIN

NEARER SPAIN

Narbo

CORSICA

Rome

Tarraco

SARDINIA

Misenum

Gades

MEDITERRANEAN

Brundisium

SICILY

MAURETANIA

Lambaesis

Carthage

Syracuse

Thapsus

NORTH

AFRICA

MAP 18
ROMAN EMPIRE UNDER AUGUSTUS

Annexed or Organized by Pompey

Annexed by Caesar

Annexed by Augustus

Scale of Miles

0   500

SARMATIANS

IAZYGES

DACIA

Danube R.

MOESIA

THRACE

Dyrrachium
Philippi

Pharsalus

Actium

Athens

BOSPORUS

Tomi

BLACK SEA

Pergamum

Smyrna

PHRYGIA

RHODES

CRETE

CYPRUS

Zela

CAPPADOCIA

CILICIA

Tarsus

Antioch
SYRIA

Damascus

ARMENIA

Carrhae

Tigris R.

PARTHIA

Ctesiphon

Seleucia

Euphrates R.

E A N   S E A

Cyrene

LIBYA

Alexandria

EGYPT

Nile R.

PALESTINE

Jerusalem

Petra

ARABIAN

DESERT

RED

SEA

CASPIAN SEA

Claudius onward they also received the prestigious grant of citizenship on discharge, inscribed on a bronze plate in Rome; each new citizen also got his own copy, a "diploma," numbers of which have survived.

Augustus and his successors thus broke with the Republican policy of raising naval forces for each specific need and judged a permanent navy desirable. Yet this navy faced no opposition in the Mediterranean for two centuries. And again, we are dealing with a people so generally and with some justice considered a landbound folk, but these same Romans developed the control and organs of sea power to their highest refinement in antiquity. Such puzzling facts insistently demand an explanation if we are to understand the Roman imperial navy; what reasons warranted to the emperors the very considerable annual expense of a far reaching naval establishment and did so through the centuries? Or, to strip the problem to its essentials, how and to what extent did the emperors judge that their power required command of the seas?

The bare statement that the Roman Empire rested on the Mediterranean, though correct, will not suffice to explain the navy:

> It is easy to say in a general way, that the use and control of the sea is and has been a great factor in the history of the world; it is more troublesome to seek out and show its exact bearing at a particular juncture. Yet, unless this be done, the acknowledgement of general importance remains vague and unsubstantial.[10]

For the first emperor, Augustus, there are reasons in abundance for his attention to the sea; the history of the dying Republic and his own rise showed clearly that the master of the Mediterranean world needed firm naval command. The squadrons which could give him that control were as a matter of fact then in existence, and had existed along with standing armies for some decades; it remained only for Augustus to give order to institutions that the half-hidden needs of the political society had already crudely formed. The demands of the civil wars had furnished the base of a permanent naval establishment just as a part of his legions and auxiliaries was organized into a standing army.

But what led his successors, not moved so directly by awareness of the importance of sea power, to maintain a standing navy across the centuries of the Early Empire? The justification, in simplest terms, may seem weak to modern military experts accustomed to cost-accounting and project evaluations: the navy was inherited, like the structure of imperial government, and the Empire was a conservative system not given to radical reforms. It could afford to support a navy without serious difficulty, just as it could provide funds to a number of emperors for huge building programs in Rome and abroad; not until the chaos of the third century did rulers have to make critical financial choices. There were, moreover, a variety of recurring services the Italian squadrons could provide for their masters, ranging from the truly useful to the whimsical, even bloodthirsty.

From the modern point of view one might think first of the protection of trade, which reached its ancient height in the Early Empire.[11] Roman aristocrats demanded marbles from every quarry as well as statues, sarcophagi, and other work in stone and metal; there was at Rome even a warehouse for pepper, an eastern luxury.[12] The population of the city itself, the largest in the world at that time, perhaps running half a million, also needed seaborne grain, a "care" the emperor Tiberius and others stressed as being much on their minds.[13] Every year a huge grain transport left Alexandria in June and returned from Puteoli and Ostia with the etesian winds in August; to facilitate its reception at the Italian end first Claudius and then Trajan created artificial harbors at Ostia where the large merchant ships could discharge their cargoes into river boats to be carried up the Tiber to Rome itself. Port installations, parenthetically, were also improved all over the Mediterranean as at Massalia and even far-off London in the late first century after Christ.[14] It is, however, unlikely that the navy had any real responsibility in patrolling this vital route; sailing ships came directly from Alexandria, but galleys could not keep to the sea for more than about 200 miles before they needed to touch shore for food and water.[15] The general peace of the Mediterranean, moreover, prevented any serious interference with seaborne trade.

If one seeks a monument to the imperial navy, it may be found in the disappearance of piracy from men's minds; as Strabo put it, sailors could be totally at ease in this respect.[16] From Augustus on to the early third century there is not one contemporary reference to a Mediterranean pirate; imperial literature has fearful portrayals of the sailor's dangers, but a swift pirate forms no part of the recital. After Labeo, in the time of Augustus, no jurist is known to have dealt with provisions of the Rhodian sea law on the subject until the third century.[17] Piracy had been eradicated from the sea lanes, a feat not repeated until the later nineteenth century after Christ. Along with the navy other factors had played their part; the peace of prosperity eliminated the buccaneering that results from disturbed political, social, or economic conditions, and the army had firmly occupied the former pirate coasts of Cilicia and Dalmatia, assisted at some points in Asia Minor and Spain by prefects of the sea coast.[18] Even at the eastern end of the Black Sea there was a guard post, "very suitable for the protection of those sailing in the area," which was further improved by Arrian.[19] Only in western Mauretania, where the mountains closely approach the sea—for some 200 miles along this coast there was not even a Roman road—could problems arise; the consequence was the seconding of detachments from the Syrian and Egyptian flotillas to Caesarea in Mauretania, under experienced officers who had already commanded auxiliary units in the region. Brigands, on the other hand, did operate on land, especially in mountainous districts away from the main Roman roads, which were reasonably well guarded; but at least once the *classis Ravennas* had to land crews to deal with troubles on the Flaminian Way.

Again, we might assume that the navy was useful in the transport of troops from frontier to frontier; for at times outbreak of hostilities with the Parthian empire on the east or the German barbarians to the north required the reenforcement of the threatened sector. Galleys, unfortunately, were not very commodious craft. Nero did send some troops by sea, but the men arrived so exhausted that they were of no immediate utility;[20] and legionary detachments had such big baggage trains that they necessarily marched by land.[21] Imperial officials and even emperors in a hurry could be transported on warships, but Titus, son of Vespasian, came to Rome in 69 on a sailing vessel; the apostle Paul and his guard also were brought thus to the capital after mishaps. Emperors did enjoy an afternoon cruise off the Tyrrhenian coast in a galley, and Nero went so far as to try to drown his mother Agrippina in a ship designed to collapse; in the end he had to order his Misene prefect to send a captain and centurion to despatch her.[22]

The real utility of the Mediterranean fleets in general military assistance was in swift despatch of letters and orders. During the second century detachments of the Italian squadrons were posted at Seleuceia in Syria several times, undoubtedly to facilitate communications; at the Italian end there were naval runners from Puteoli and Ostia to Rome, where both flotillas had separate barracks. Sailors also, we are incidentally informed, manipulated the awnings in the Colosseum, and Claudius had the Misene fleet plant oysters along the Campanian coast.[23]

At least once in the Early Empire the essential military role of the Mediterranean fleets became more visible. The last emperor descended from Augustus and Livia, Nero, lost the support of the Senate, the urban masses, and the armies by his erratic tyranny and dissolute ways of life; in 68 he had to commit suicide as rebellious troops were advancing on Rome. Civil war followed, in which ambitious field commanders vied for the purple. Vespasian, erstwhile governor of Syria, was victor both by reason of his own ability and the cooperation of the Balkan generals; but a minor, yet important factor was the support of the Italian squadrons and his control of the food supplies provided to Rome from Egypt. In his reign the navy reached its apogee. Naval prefects now held a much higher rank in the equestrian hierarchy, and both Italian squadrons received the honorary title *praetoria*. Among the representations of victory on his coinage only one has a specific description, Victoria Navalis, in clear reference to the role of sea power in giving him success.[24] Thereafter the Empire passed through decades of internal peace until the end of the second century, when civil war was again to erupt.

Conditions were not always as quiet on the frontiers. In Europe Augustus had pushed Roman control to the Rhine and Danube and even beyond; here naval power had very significant military utility. Already in the German campaigns of Drusus and Tiberius, sons of Augustus' wife Livia, ships played an important role on the Rhine and gave rise to the *classis Germanica;* after southern Britain was conquered under Claudius a *classis Britannica* provided a safe link between Gesoriacum (Boulogne) and several south English ports. On the Danube there appeared eventually the *classis Pannonica* on its upper reaches and the *classis Moesica* downstream. During the reign of Nero the subject kingdom of Pontus on the north coast of Asia Minor was annexed in connection with the Armenian wars of the period, and the *classis Pontica* was created out of the former royal navy. The ships in these fleets were of lighter build than conventional triremes but carried out their tasks efficiently; their bases were *castra* structured much as army posts.[25]

In peacetime the galleys patrolled their rivers to ensure that barbarians came across to trade only at designated points; to keep the manpower busy sailors also made bricks for forts and in Britain worked in iron mines and on Hadrian's Wall. During military activity they were even more useful. In campaigns across the Rhine to keep the Germans divided the army often moved in parallel columns to fix the fugitive enemy; while doing so it was aided by the *classis Germanica* at its back, which also operated up tributary rivers and even the North Sea, as Augustus proudly boasted.[26]

The wars by which Trajan early in the second century conquered Dacia, the modern Romania, are graphically illustrated in the frieze on his column in Rome. The curtain rises quietly on a countryside of the Danube with the riverbank *castella* that the Moesian fleet linked into a chain of defense, but immediately the tale passes to a portrayal of ships laden with barrels and soldiers' packs, which are being put on shore at a town—preparation for war. This scene, recurring at intervals throughout the early part of the reliefs, marks the usefulness of the *classis Moesica* in the maintenance of the army, for which the Danube furnished an incomparable route.[27] The galleys themselves could not transport the materials of war, and on the Column the freight ships are clearly distinguished from warships; the main service of the latter, and a sufficient one, was in so dominating the river that this supply might proceed uninterrupted. After the final victory the task of patrolling the lowlands east of the Dacian hills was entrusted to auxiliary units backed by the *classis Moesica*.

During the reign of the philosopher king Marcus Aurelius (161–80) signs of trouble became more evident internally and externally. The population of the Empire was beginning to shrink and was more openly divided into upper and lower classes; the prosperity of the cities was also declining, and imperial revenues were heavily stressed by the long continued wars on the northern frontiers. In 170 a barbarian tribe, the Costoboci, broke through the Danube defenses and penetrated as far as Greece; to counter this threat the *classis Pontica* was shifted from Trapezus to Cyzicus, where it could firmly control the Hellespont; and a prefect of extraordinary rank was for a time appointed. The Moors ventured from 171–72 onward to ravage more widely in the Mediterranean; the emperor took over direct responsibility for southern Spain and sent an imperial officer, presumably with the aid of the Misene fleet and perhaps even of the Ravennate squadron, to chase them back to their lairs. The temporary inability of imperial military and naval forces to put down rebellious subjects in the Mediterranean itself was an evil omen, but not in itself disastrous.

After the assassination of Marcus Aurelius' unworthy son Commodus in 192 civil war again broke out, as in 68–69, when generals contended for the succession. A civilian aristocrat, Didius Julianus, bought the throne by huge gifts to the praetorian guard, but his rule was short. The Ravennate fleet, despite the efforts of Didius to strengthen its loyalty, deserted to Septimius Severus, governor of Syria, as he entered Italy. Misene sailors whom Didius summoned to Rome proved as untrustworthy; the historian Dio Cassius, then in Rome, jeered at their sorry military training.[28]

The Mediterranean squadrons were of great value even so to Septimius Severus in his war against another claimant, Pescennius Niger. While Septimius Severus moved east by land, the navy transported part of his forces to the Balkans at Dyrrachium and then in the Aegean probably helped the crossing into Asia Minor, where Niger was crushed. Most of the navy then remained in the east to aid in the siege of Byzantium, which had declared for

Niger and held out after his suicide until the winter of 195–96. One official of the Misene fleet rendered such good service that Septimius Severus took the unprecedented step of advancing him to the Senate and promoted him steadily thereafter. In Septimius Severus' last years he campaigned along the northern coasts of Britain with the *classis Britannica* in support.

On his death in 211 the complex geographical and administrative frame of imperial sea power still stood in its entirety. The fleets grew older decade by decade without fundamental change; ancient discipline trained anew recruits to fill the ranks of discharged veterans; the dockyards replaced worn-out vessels with new; prefect succeeded prefect in the unending, unvarying wheel of administration. Hardened tradition carried the navy on and enabled it to meet the stresses of 193; the siege of Byzantium indicated that the imperial fleets still controlled the Mediterranean. The greater upheavals to come, nonetheless, were to show that imperial appreciation of sea power had slowly diminished; the shrinking resources of the empire had to be devoted rather to desperate efforts at maintaining military strength.

During the third century every type of political and natural calamity, including a great plague, weakened the imperial structure. Pretenders to the throne rose freely, and few real emperors had reigns of any length. On the east the Sassanian dynasty, which had supplanted the ineffectual Parthians, was a far more serious threat and at times advanced as far as Asia Minor. During the first half of the third century the Italian squadrons continued to perform their usual functions in eastern campaigns. In 214 an accident sank Caracalla's galley in crossing the northern Aegean, but he was saved by an unnamed naval prefect; and as late as Gordan III (238–44) the emperor moved east by sea at least part of the way.[29]

On the northern frontier the barbarians, now often partly civilized by long contact with Roman traders, grouped themselves in larger units and repeatedly broke the Roman defenses. From about 254 on to 269 the Goths ravaged the eastern provinces, at first by land and then by sea; in one foray they were reported to have had 500 light vessels. Their attacks were defeated primarily on land, but naval forces of some type did meet and stop the naval threat in battles off Rhodes, Crete, and Cyprus.

The Italian fleets could have given scant assistance against the Goths, for they were fully committed in the western Mediterranean under admirals appointed ad hoc to control the shores as well. Their limited success is illuminated by the extraordinary voyage of some Franks settled in Thrace, who seized vessels and made their way through the Mediterranean and the strait of Gibraltar to return to their homeland. Everywhere piracy again became a curse to those who ventured on the seas.

Of the 10 squadrons in existence in 230 only three remained when Diocletian became emperor at Nicomedia in 284 and restored financial, military, and political order to the badly shaken Roman world. His efforts and those of his coadjutors were directed to the restoration of the frontiers and the consolidation of a system of mobile field armies, using far more cavalry than in earlier centuries. Diocletian is often compared to Augustus, but he did not devote any significant attention to the sea. Mediterranean commerce had so declined that its protection became less openly essential, and the Late Empire, as the state organized by Diocletian is known, had no funds for the unessential. Even more important, Augustus had at his disposal a navy already in existence; Diocletian succeeded to a period in which the navy had largely been destroyed. Evidence for the Italian squadrons does continue for a time, but more and more naval activity rested on temporary flotillas recruited for the occasion, as had been the practice in late Republican times. In the duel between Constantine and Licinius in 323–24 the former had 200 warships equipped at Thessalonica and with them won the only real sea battle in the history of the Roman Empire.[30] Emperors might be hailed as "masters of land and sea," but the term was only conventional.[31]

One provincial flotilla, the *classis Britannica*, did have a brief day of glory in Diocletian's time. By 285 the Franks and Saxons had begun the raids along the English Channel which continued until they became settlers and rulers in the fifth century. That, however, was not yet to be, for Diocletian quickly took steps to check this and other unrest in the west. His assistant in the area,

Maximian, appointed an army officer, Carausius, to command the fleet at Gesoriacum; after initial successes Carausius revolted and claimed the title of emperor himself on the base of British allegiance. On his coins symbols of naval power such as galleys appear, and he guarded his realm for several years until his murder by his chief aide. By this time another deputy of Diocletian, Constantius Chlorus, father of Constantine, had built a fleet and restored central authority over Britain, thus ending the only occasion during the Roman Empire when an usurper rested his rule on sea power.

Later in the century, probably about 370, an anonymous author wrote a pamphlet for the emperors of the time advising them how to save money and improve military defense by a variety of ingenious inventions. One of these was a warship propelled by oxen hitched to wheels on the side of the galley that acted like oars. "Owing to its massiveness and the machines working inside it," the vessel "joins battle with such furious strength that it easily crushes and destroys all opposing warships that come to close quarters with it."[32] The possibility of naval encounters is clearly envisaged, but there were actually no more naval battles in the ancient Mediterranean; needless to say the craft was never built, and its very suggestion shows how completely organized naval strength had vanished.

During the long deterioration of Roman rule in the western parts of Europe and Africa, the Decline and Fall which ended in 476, civil wars and barbarian invasions took place not on the sea but on land.[33] The desperate emperors of the fifth century, hidden in the impregnable fortress of Ravenna, sought to appease the invading German tribes by assigning them tracts of land where they took over usually half the territory, but it is noticeable that in their grants the barbarians were carefully kept away from the seacoast, which still supported some commerce; imperial edicts even banned training the Germans in the building of ships.[34]

These efforts were in vain. In 429 the able leader of the Vandals, Gaiseric, led his people across the strait of Gibraltar to Africa, where he secured Carthage in 439 and was reluctantly recognized by the Empire as independent in 442. Gaiseric became strong enough on the sea to attack Rome in 455 and sack it; there was no Misene fleet to counter him on open waters.[35] Almost exactly 600 years earlier, when Scipio Aemilianus accepted the surrender of Carthage (146 B.C.), the great Roman aristocrat had turned to his friend, the historian Polybius, and voiced his "dread foreboding that some day the same doom will be pronounced upon my own country."[36] The ghost of Hannibal could have looked down on Gaiseric's Vandals in Rome and smiled.

Although the western provinces thus slipped out of central control, the eastern parts of the Mediterranean world, based on the enduring strength of the Greek cities, continued to nourish imperial power in the Byzantine state, ruled from the great capital of Constantinople. Its emperors had reason to pay attention to the sea as well as to the land; a Byzantine fleet was to be invaluable in helping defeat Arab attacks after the rise of Islam. In the west travel was once again as insecure as it had been in the second millennium B.C., and conditions were not to be improved over the next thousand years.

Epilogue

Since the promulgation of Mahan's theory the role of sea power has generally been considered decisive in the history of the modern world and by extension in antiquity at several turning points. Yet acceptance has not been complete; in particular the famous British geographer, Sir Halford Mackinder, argued in *Democratic Ideals and Reality,* published just after World War I, that control of the great landmass of Eurasia was, or could be, far more significant. This view he summed up in the jingle:

> Who rules East Europe commands the Heartland;
> Who rules the Heartland commands the World-Island
> Who rules the World-Island commands the World.[1]

German geopoliticians, including Haushofer, leaned heavily on Mackinder's concept, which thus enjoyed some authority in Nazi times; but otherwise it seems to have sunk into relative obscurity.[2]

In ancient history two states rested their position primarily on the sea. Carthage dominated the western Mediterranean for centuries, with considerable political and economic effects, but it is not clear that Carthage could ever have been a cultural leader, as Rome was to be, even though it was much affected by Hellenistic civilization.[3] The other, the Athenian naval empire, has long been taken as a paradigm of the utility of rule of the sea. Here too the political and economic consequences were significant, but we must also reckon into the balance sheet the cultural advances that have influenced Western civilization ever since the great days of Athens.

Both, however, were crushed by states primarily powerful on land. True, Rome and Sparta had to go to sea and gain naval mastery over their opponents, but under the surface the strengths of organization and determination as perfected on land were decisive in their success. Finally, as we have just seen, the Roman Empire produced the most conscious and widely based organization of naval strength to protect the prosperity of an age later hailed as the "most happy" in the history of the human race.[4] The eventual deterioration of the navy was, even so, not the principal factor in the Decline and Fall.

The strengths, the weaknesses, and the ultimate values of sea power are well and diversely illuminated in the ancient world; what lessons we may draw from this experience it is not for an ancient historian to presume to suggest. It would be well, nonetheless, to keep in mind Mackinder as well as Mahan.

Notes

Introduction

1. *From Sail to Steam* (New York, 1907), p. 277.
2. *History of Rome,* Book 3, chap. 4.
3. W. D. Puleston, *Mahan* (New Haven, 1933), p. 159; R. B. Downs, *Books that Changed the World* (2d ed.; Chicago, 1978), pp. 252–62.
4. R. Meiggs, *Trees and Timber in the Ancient Mediterranean World* (Oxford, 1982), p. 117.
5. Strabo 1. 1. 6 C8, 8. 1. 3 C334, so too 9. 2, 21 C408 in describing Thessaly.
6. Appian, *Roman History* 8. 87.
7. J. F. Matthews, *Journal of Roman Studies* 74 (1984), p. 170.
8. As asserted by A. Lesky, *Thalatta: Der Weg der Griechen zum Meer* (Vienna, 1947), p. 41, "Auf der Schiffahrt beruhten Macht und Wohlstand." Among the many treatments of ancient trade, see recently *Trade in the Ancient Economy,* edd. P. D. A. Garnsey, K. Hopkins, and C. R. Whittaker (Berkeley, 1983).
9. John Masefield, *Cargoes.*
10. T. J. Figuera, *American Journal of Philology* 106 (1985), p. 64.
11. See, for example, the works of Casson, Meijer, Morrison, and Rougé listed in the Bibliography.
12. Here I may note that studies of naval power in modern history such as L. W. Martin, *The Sea in Modern Strategy* (London, 1967), are not very useful though at times they do suggest its limitations (so P. M. Kennedy, *The Rise and Fall of British Naval Mastery* [London, 1976]). A. R. Lewis and T. J. Runyan, *European Naval and Maritime History 300–1500* (Bloomington, Indiana, 1985), argue that sea power held together empires in this long period but admit

that the decisive battles were usually on land; not until the sixteenth century did naval conflicts such as Lepanto and the Spanish
Armada have significant consequences.

Chapter I

1. Strabo 1. 3. 4 C49; F. Meijer, *A History of Seafaring in the Classical
   World* (New York, 1986), p. 29, has a map of the currents.
2. B. W. Labaree, "How The Greeks Sailed into the Black Sea," *American Journal of Archaeology* 61 (1957), pp. 29–33.
3. So Strabo 2. 5. 18 C122ff. subdivides the Mediterranean.
4. K. Honea, "Prehistoric Remains on the Island of Kythnos," *American Journal of Archaeology* 79 (1975), pp. 277–79.
5. Most recently E. A. Fisher, *American Journal of Archaeology* 89
   (1985), p. 330; but note the caution of R. Ross Holloway, *Italy and
   the Aegean, 3000–700 B.C.* (Louvain, 1981), p. 89.
6. On the growth of this trade see J. Bouzek, *The Aegean, Anatolia
   and Europe: Cultural Interrelations in the Second Millennium B. C.*
   (Göteborg, 1985).
7. G. F. Bass, "A Bronze Age Shipwreck at Ulu Buṛun (Kaş): 1985
   Campaign," *American Journal of Archaeology* 90 (1986), pp. 264–
   96, and a brief report on the 1986 campaign 91 (1987), p. 321; also
   the well illustrated survey in *National Geographic*, December 1987,
   pp. 693–732.
8. F. Braudel, *The Mediterranean and the Mediterranean World in
   the Age of Philip II* (New York, 1973), p. 296, cf. pp. 122–23; J. F.
   Shepherd and G. M. Walton, *Shipping, Maritime Trade, and the
   Economic Development of Colonial North America* (Cambridge,
   1972), p. 196; according to L. Casson, *Ships and Seamanship in the
   Ancient World* (Princeton, 1971), pp. 171–72, sailing ships still ran
   70 to 150 tons in classical times.
9. S. Marinatos, "La Marine Créto-Mycénienne" *Bulletin de Corre-
   spondance Hellénique* 57 (1933), pp. 170–235.
10. A. T. Mahan, *The Influence of Sea Power upon the French Revolu-
    tion and Empire* (Boston, 1918), p. 152; cf. Braudel, I, pp. 358–74,
    on the variation in time for various voyages.
11. P. Warren, "The Miniature Fresco from the West House at Akro-
    tiri, Thera, and its Aegean Setting," *Journal of Hellenic Studies*
    99 (1979), pp. 115–29; A. Raban, "The Thera Ships: Another In-
    terpretation," *American Journal of Archaeology* 88 (1984), pp.
    11–19.

12. Warren, pp. 128–29, is ambiguous as to whether the raiders depicted in the Thera fresco are Mycenaean or Minoan but is willing to believe that Minoans themselves could raid. See my reevaluation of their "peaceful" ways in "Minoan Flower Lovers," *The Minoan Thalassocracy: Myth and Reality* (Stockholm, 1984), pp. 9–12.

13. T. Säve-Söderbergh, *The Navy of the Eighteenth Egyptian Dynasty* (Uppsala, 1946).

14. S. R. K. Glanville, *Zeitschrift für Ägyptische Sprache und Altertumskunde* 66 (1930), p. 109, on the Memphis dockyard.

15. Thucydides 1. 4; Herodotus 3. 122; Strabo 10. 4. 8 C476; Diodorus Siculus 5. 78. See generally my "Myth of the Minoan Thalassocracy," *Historia* 3 (1955), pp. 282–91 (now in my *Essays on Ancient History* [Leiden, 1979]), pp. 87–96). I adhere to the views there expressed despite the counter by R. J. Buck, "The Minoan Thalassocracy Re-examined," *Historia* 11 (1962), pp. 129–37. The essays in *The Minoan Thalassocracy: Myth or Reality* are largely archeologically oriented.

16. L. Casson, *The Ancient Mariners* (New York, 1959), p. 29.

17. Cf. F. T. Jane, *The British Battle Fleet,* 1 (2d ed.; London, 1915), pp. 6–7.

18. H. J. Kantor, *The Aegean and the Orient in the Second Millennium B. C.* (Bloomington, Ind., 1947), p. 54.

19. L. Cohen, "Evidence for the Ram in the Minoan Period," *American Journal of Archaeology* 42 (1938), pp. 486–94; J. S. Morrison and R. T. Williams, *Greek Oared Ships 900–322 B. C.* (Cambridge, 1968), p. 7, still invest Mycenaean ships with short rams, but see Casson, *Ships and Seamanship,* pp. 41–42, 49ff.

20. J. B. Pritchard, *Ancient Near Eastern Texts Relating to the Old Testament* (Princeton, 1950), p. 262.

21. H. Nelson, "The Naval Battle Pictured at Medinet Habu," *Journal of Near Eastern Studies* 2 (1943), pp. 40–55; S. Wachsmann, "The Ships of the Sea Peoples," *International Journal of Nautical Archaeology* 10 (1981), pp. 187–220; see generally N. K. Sandars, *The Sea Peoples: Warriors of the Ancient Mediterranean 1250–1150 B. C.* (2d ed.; London, 1985).

22. Pritchard, *Ancient Near Eastern Texts,* pp. 25–29.

Chapter II

1. J. Collis, *The European Iron Age* (London, 1984), provides a brief overview of the effects in the west of renewed contacts with the

east; see also the detailed and thoughtful synthesis by R. Ross Holloway, *Italy and the Aegean, 3000–700 B. C.* (Louvain, 1981).

2. F. G. Niemeyer, ed., *Die Phönizier im Westen* (Mainz, 1982); B. H. Warmington, *Carthage* (London, 1960).

3. D. Ridgway, *L'Alba della Magna Grecia* (Milan, 1984).

4. S. Humphreys, *Parola del Passato* 22 (1967), pp. 384–85.

5. See generally my *Economic and Social Growth of Early Greece 800–500 B.C.* (New York, 1977); *Individual and Community: The Rise of the Polis 800–500 B.C.* (New York, 1986).

6. Dio Chrysostom, *Orations* 36. 5.

7. *Works and Days* 646ff.

8. *Oxford Book of Greek Verse* (Oxford, 1953), p. 572.

9. Leskey, *Thalatta: Der Weg der Griechen zum Meer,* passim.

10. T. S. Noonan, "The Grain Trade of the Northern Black Sea in Antiquity," *American Journal of Philology* 94 (1973), pp. 231–42; C. A. Roebuck, "The Grain Trade between Greece and Egypt," *Classical Philology* 45 (1950), pp. 236–47, and "The Economic Development of Ionia," *Classical Philology* 48 (1953), pp. 9–16.

11. *Odyssey* 8. 159–64; my *Economic and Social Growth,* pp. 46–54, and *Past and Future in Ancient History* (Lanham, Maryland, 1987), pp. 16–17. Holloway, *Italy and the Aegean,* pp. 47–49, has an interesting view of early exchanges.

12. Herodotus 4. 196.

13. Herodotus 4. 152.

14. *Iliad* 6. 236.

15. Casson, *The Ancient Mariners,* p. 87, emphasizes the "graceful form and superb lines" of ancient sailing ships against the common view that they were not very reliable tubs; see also C. H. Ericsson, *Navis Oneraria* (Åbo, 1984), and on tonnage H. T. Wallinga, "Nautika I," *Mnemosyne* 17 (1964), pp. 1–40.

16. N. M. Verdelis, "Der Diolkos am Isthmus von Korinth," *Athenische Mitteilungen* 71 (1951), pp. 51–59; B. R. MacDonald, "The Diolkos," *Journal of Hellenic Studies* 106 (1986), pp. 191–95.

17. R. Güngerich, *Die Küstenbeschreibung in der griechischen Literatur* (Münster, 1950).

18. A. M. Snodgrass, *Trade in the Ancient Economy,* pp. 16–17, goes so far as to argue that early trade was conducted via pentekonters, but see C. Reed, *Ancient World* 10 (1984), pp. 39–41.

19. *Odyssey* 9. 40–42; in 14. 249ff. such a raid fails.

20. G. Ahlberg, *Fighting on Land and Sea in Greek Geometric Art* (Stockholm, 1971).

21. M. Gras, "A propos de la 'bataille d'Alalia'," *Latomus* 31 (1972), pp. 698–716.

22. Morrison and Williams, *Greek Oared Ships,* pp. 181–83.

23. So L. Basch, "Phoenician Oared Ships," *The Mariner's Mirror* 55 (1969), pp. 139–62, 227–46; *Journal of Hellenic Studies* 97 (1977), pp. 1–10 and 100 (1980), pp. 198–99; countered by A. B. Lloyd, "Were Necho's Triremes Phoenician?" *Journal of Hellenic Studies* 95 (1975), pp. 45–61 and 100 (1980), pp. 195–98. A vital question that never seems to be raised is *why* either Greeks or Phoenicians developed the warship equipped with a ram and several banks of oars. I point out the question only here because the answer is far from clear. True naval battles do not occur until the sixth century as far as our evidence goes; were there earlier skirmishes off Cyprus or elsewhere?

24. Thucydides 1. 14. A. Degani, *Studi su Ipponatta* (Bari, 1984), would lower Hipponax to the reign of Darius.

25. Most recently J. S. Morrison and J. F. Coates, *The Athenian Trireme: The History and Reconstruction of an Ancient Greek Warship* (Cambridge, 1986). I have not seen J. F. Coates and S. McGrail, edd., *The Greek Trireme of the 5th Century B.C.* (London, 1985), or A. W. Sleeswyck, "A New Reconstruction of the Attic Triere and Bireme," *International Journal of Naval Archaeology* 11 (1982), pp. 35–46.

26. Lucan, *Pharsalia* 3. 647–52.

27. A. W. Gomme, "A Forgotten Factor in Greek Naval Strategy," *Journal of Hellenic Studies* 53 (1933), pp. 16–24; Thucydides 1. 48; Xenophon, *Hellenica* 6. 2, gives a good description of care in landing by night in hostile territory; in Demosthenes, *Oration* 50, Apollodorus describes the discomfort when ships had to ride at anchor all night.

28. W. W. Tarn, "Fleet Speeds," *Classical Review* 23 (1909), pp. 184–86.

29. Morrison and Coates, *Athenian Trireme,* p. 197, suggest that the maximum wave a trireme could take was about 0.85 m.

30. Appian, *Civil Wars* 2. 59; cf. Xenophon, *Hellenica* 6. 2, on a blockade of Corcyra "when the weather permitted," and the difficulties of the Athenians at Pylos (Thucydides 4. 26–27).

31. E.g., Herodotus 6. 17; J. Taillardat, "La triére athénienne et la guerre sur mer," *Problèmes de la guerre en Grèce ancienne,* ed. J. P. Vernant (Paris, 1968), pp. 183–205.

32. Herodotus 7. 9.

33. Casson, *Ships,* p. 49.

34. Herodotus 1. 166.
35. Thucydides 2. 89; one of the best pictures of naval tactics is in
    Polybius 16. 2–7, describing the battle of Chios in 201. See generally
    on naval maneuvers H. T. Wallinga, *The Boarding-Bridge of the
    Romans* (Groningen, 1956), ch. 5, and J. S. Morrison, "Greek Naval
    Tactics in the 5th Century B.C.," *International Journal of Naval
    Archaeology* 3 (1974), pp. 21–26.
36. W. L. Rodgers, *Greek and Roman Naval Warfare* (Annapolis, 1937),
    pp. 131–33.
37. Thucydides 4. 32, however, suggests that rowers were not regularly
    equipped with arms; on occasion hoplites served as rowers so that a
    full armed force could be landed (Thucydides 3. 18, 8.24).
38. Against B. Jordan, *The Athenian Navy in the Classical Period*
    (Berkeley, 1975), pp. 260ff., see J. S. Morrison, *Journal of Hellenic
    Studies* 104 (1984), pp. 48–59.
39. My *Individual and Community*, pp. 46–47.
40. Casson, *Ships*, pp. 90–91, puts the life of a trireme at 20 years on
    the average; the wreck of a sailing ship from the fourth century
    was estimated to have been more than 80 years old (M. L. Katsev,
    National Geographic 137 [1970], p. 856).
41. Herodotus 3. 19.
42. M. G. Ientile, *La pirateria tirrenica (Kokalos,* Suppl. 6; Rome,
    1983); M. Cristofani, *Gli Etruschi del Mare* (Milan, 1983); cf. the
    exploits in the fifth century of Velthus Spurinna recorded in his
    elogium at Tarquinia (M. Torelli, *Elogia Tarquiniensia* [Florence,
    1975], pp. 56–66).
43. J. M. Turffa, "Evidence for Etruscan-Punic Relations," *American
    Journal of Archaeology* 81 (1977), pp. 368–74.
44. See my *Beginnings of Imperial Rome* (Ann Arbor, 1980), pp. 33–34.
45. Herodotus 1. 143.
46. Herodotus 4. 44; see recently the careful essay by H. T. Wallinga,
    "The Ancient Persian Navy and its Predecessors," *Archaemenid
    History* 1 (Leiden, 1987), pp. 47–77.
47. Thucydides 1. 15.
48. Herodotus 3. 39ff., 3. 122.
49. Ps.-Plato, *Hipparchus* 228c.
50. M. M. Eisman, "Attic Kyathos Production," *Archaeology* 28 (1975),
    pp. 76–83.
51. Most recently R. Thomsen, *Eisphora* (Copenhagen, 1964), pp. 120ff.
52. Herodotus 6. 89, 6. 92–93; C. J. Haas, "Athenian Naval Power be-
    fore Themistocles," *Historia* 34 (1985), pp. 29–46.

53. Herodotus 6. 39, 6. 41, 5. 97.
54. Thucydides 7. 21.

Chapter III

1. Herodotus 5. 97. There is no need here to footnote the history of Athens and of Greece generally in the fifth and fourth centuries; a sound guide is E. Will, *Le Monde grec et l'Orient; le Ve siècle* (Paris, 1971), and the companion volume on the fourth century (largely by C. Mossé, Paris, 1975). In English N. G. L. Hammond, *History of Greece to 322 B.C.* (2d ed.; Oxford, 1977), is detailed.

2. H. T. Wallinga, "The Ionian Revolt," *Mnemosyne* 37 (1984), pp. 401–37; D. Lateiner, "The Failure of the Ionian Revolt," *Historia* 31 (1982), pp. 129–60; P. Tozzi, *La rivolta ionica* (Pisa, 1978).

3. D. F. Graf, "Medism," *Journal of Hellenic Studies* 104 (1984), pp. 15–30.

4. Thucydides 1. 93; J. LaBarbe, *La Loi navale de Thémistocle* (Paris, 1957).

5. Meiggs, *Trees,* pp. 122–25.

6. Plutarch, *Cimon* 12.

7. Thucydides 1. 74.

8. Herodotus 8. 1, 8. 44, 8. 46.

9. Herodotus 7. 139; cf, earlier the comments by Artabanus on the role of the sea, 7. 10, 7. 49.

10. Thucydides 1. 95, placed in perspective by R. Meiggs, *The Athenian Empire* (Oxford, 1972), pp. 40–43.

11. W. S. Ferguson, *Greek Imperialism* (Boston, 1913), p. 74; see also W. Schuller, *Die Herrschaft der Athener im ersten Attischen Seebund* (Berlin, 1974). In following pages I have drawn occasionally on my essay, "Athens and Its Empire," delivered at the Library of Congress in November 1986 and published in *Classical Journal* 83 (1988), pp. 114–23.

12. J. Flint, *Cecil Rhodes* (Boston, 1974), pp. 228–29; J. Schumpeter, "The Sociology of Imperialism," *Imperialism and Social Classes* (New York, 1955), pp. 3–98; W. V. Harris, *War and Imperialism in Republican Rome 327–70 B.C.* (Oxford, 1978), pp. 30ff.

13. J. de Romilly, *Thucydides and Athenian Imperialism* (Oxford, 1963), p. 79; on pp. 71–73 she efficiently discounts the efforts of G. B. Grundy and others to find economic motives for Athenian imperialism.

14. Thucydides 1. 120. G. E. M. de Ste Croix, *The Origins of the Pelo-*

ponnesian War (Oxford, 1972), c. 7, is full on the Megarian decree though he distorts its bearing and terms.

15. Ferguson, *Greek Imperialism,* pp. 42–43.

16. F. Frost, *American Journal of Ancient History* 1 (1976), p. 70; on gangs, Demosthenes, *Oration* 32. 10.

17. Eupolis, quoted by Dio Chrysostom, *Oration* 64. 16; F. Koch, *Comicorum Atticorum Fragmenta* 1 (Leipzig, 1880), adesp. 344.

18. See my essay on "Thucydides on Sea Power," *Mnemosyne* 31 (1979), pp. 343–50.

19. Plutarch, *Themistocles* 4. 3; *Die Fragmente der griechischen Historiker,* ed. F. Jacoby, 2. B (Leiden, 1962), 107. 2. A. Momigliano, "Sea Power in Greek Thought," *Secondo Contributo* (Rome, 1966), pp. 52–67, treats primarily moral aspects as viewed by fourth-century authors.

20. Thucydides 2. 60–64; R. Garland, *The Piraeus* (Ithaca, 1987), pp. 18ff.

21. The change is discussed in my *Athenian Coinage 480–449 B.C.* (Oxford, 1970), pp. 64–71.

22. B. D. Meritt, H. T. Wade-Gery, and M. F. McGregor, *The Athenian Tribute Lists,* 4 vols. (Cambridge, Mass., 1939–53), is the fundamental publication of this evidence.

23. Meijer, *History of Seafaring,* p. 69, estimates annual pay of the navy at about 480 talents; each year moreover 20 to 30 new ships had to be built at a cost of 30 to 50 talents; repairs, dockyard expense, and other items must also be added to the list. See also S. K. Eddy, "Athens' Peacetime Navy in the Age of Pericles," *Greek Roman and Byzantine Studies* 9 (1968), pp. 144–56.

24. E.g., Thucydides 1. 31, 1. 35, 1. 121, 1. 143, 6. 22, 6. 43, 7. 13, 7. 57. Drafting: Thucydides 7. 13.

25. G. E. M. de Ste Croix, "Jurisdiction in the Athenian Empire," *Classical Quarterly* 11 (1961), pp. 94–112, 268–80.

26. M. Ostwald, *Autonomia: Its Genesis and Early History* (Scholars Press, 1982); V. Ehrenberg, *The Greek State* (Oxford, 1960).

27. G. E. M. de Ste Croix, "The Character of the Athenian Empire," *Historia* 3 (1954–55), pp. 1–41; promptly rebutted by H. B. Mattingly, *Historia* 12 (1963), pp. 257–73; T. J. Quinn, *Historia* 13 (1964), pp. 257–66; D. W. Bradeen, *Historia* 9 (1960), pp. 257–69; H. W. Pleket, *Historia* 12 (1963), pp. 70–77.

28. *British Documents on the Origins of the War, 1898–1914,* ed. G. P. Gooch and H. Temperley, 3 (London, 1928), pp. 402–3, a memorandum of January 1, 1907.

29. On privateering see Thucydides 2. 67, 2. 69, 2. 93, 3. 2, 4. 5, 4. 53, 8. 35.

30. Thucydides 6. 34.

31. Thucydides 8. 96.

32. J. K. Davies, *Wealth and the Power of Wealth in Classical Athens* (Oxford, 1981), pp. 20–21; A. Boeckh, *Die Staatshaushaltung der Athener* (3d ed.; Munich, 1886), first explored in depth the fourth-century naval inventories; there were apparently more general inventories in the fifth century.

33. A. Andreades, *A History of Greek Public Finance*, 1 (Cambridge, Mass., 1933), p. 243; Xenophon, *Hellenica* 4. 8, 5. 1, 5. 4; Demosthenes, *Oration* 50.

34. S. Humphreys, *The Craft of the Ancient Historian*, edd. J. Eadie and J. Ober (Lanham, Maryland, 1985), p. 225.

35. Xenophon, *Hellenica* 7. 1 (but in 6. 1 Jason argues that Thessaly had greater resources of timber, men, and grain for naval power).

36. Davies, *Wealth*, pp. 13ff.; J. Amit, *Athens and the Sea* (Brussels, 1965), pp. 103–15; J. Cargill, *The Second Athenian League* (Berkeley, 1981).

37. Herodotus 8. 17; so too Philip of Croton in the late sixth century had his own trireme (Herodotus 5. 47); cf. Jordan, *Athenian Navy*, p. 91.

38. Jordan, *Athenian Navy*, pp. 70–83.

39. Demosthenes, *Oration* 50.

40. F. J. Maroon and E. L. Beach, *Keepers of the Sea* (Annapolis, 1983), p. 17.

41. Arrian, *Anabasis* 7. 19.

42. It may be noted here that I have passed over a list of ancient thalassocracies, first known from Castor of Rhodes and preserved in Eusebius, as being totally fictitious, despite M. Miller, *The Thalassocracies* (Albany, 1971); see the bibliography in L. H. Jeffery, *Archaic Greece* (London, 1976), pp. 252–53. The most recent treatment of the end of Athenian naval strength is J. S. Morrison, "Athenian Sea-power in 323/2 BC," *Journal of Hellenic Studies* 107 (1987), pp. 88–97.

Chapter IV

1. On Hellenistic history see the thorough study by E. Will, *Histoire politique du monde hellénistique*, 2 vols. (2d ed.; Nancy, 1979 and 1982); the brief remarks by W. W. Tarn, *Hellenistic Military and*

Naval Developments (Cambridge, 1930). For the Ptolemaic empire, R. S. Bagnall, *The Administration of the Ptolemaic Possessions outside Egypt* (Leiden, 1971); I. Merker, *Historia* 19 (1970), pp. 141–60.

2. Diodorus 20. 47–52; E. Gruen, in *The Craft of the Ancient Historian*, p. 255.

3. Tarn, *Developments*, pp. 122–41; on the Venetian system my "Ancient Warship," *Classical Philology* 35 (1940), pp. 353–74, esp. pp. 371ff. (now in my *Essays on Ancient History*, pp. 59–80); L. Casson, "The Super-galleys of the Hellenistic World," *The Mariner's Mirror* 55 (1969), pp. 185–93; R. Anderson, *Oared Fighting Ships* (London, 1962), pp. 21–30, provides the alternative explanation.

4. Polybius 1. 26. 7; on Athenian building N. G. Ashton, "How Many Pentereis?" *Greek Roman and Byzantine Studies* 20 (1979), pp. 237–42. The difficulties triremes faced in attacking quinqueremes are well illustrated by the story in Polybius 15. 2.

5. Morrison, *Athenian Trireme*, p. 48; see generally E. W. Marsden, *Greek and Roman Artillery* (Oxford, 1969).

6. Will, *Histoire politique*, I, pp. 134–37, 159–78; L. Casson, "The Grain Trade of the Hellenistic World," *Transactions of the American Philological Association* 85 (1954), pp. 168–87.

7. Pausanias 3. 6. 5; A. Bouché-Leclercq, *Histoire des Lagides*, 4 (Paris, 1907), p. 7; Will, *Cambridge Ancient History*, 7. 1 (Cambridge, 1984). See generally R. S. Bagnall, "The Ptolemaic Trierarchs," *Chronique d'Égypte* 46 (1971), pp. 356–62; H. Hauben, "Callicrates of Samos," *Studia hellenistica* 18 (1970); J. Lesquier, *Les institutions militaires de l'Égypte sous les Lagides* (Paris, 1911).

8. F. W. Walbank, *Journal of Roman Studies* 106 (1986), p. 243, reviewing K. Buraselis, *Das hellenistische Makedonien und die Ägäis* (Munich, 1983).

9. M. Bieber, *Sculpture of the Hellenistic Age* (rev. ed.; New York, 1961), pp. 125–26.

10. Tarn, *Developments*, p. 142.

11. Polybius 4. 46–47; Strabo 14. 2. 5 C651; R. M. Berthold, *Rhodes in the Hellenistic World* (Ithaca, 1984).

12. Polybius 5. 89.

13. See my *Beginnings of Imperial Rome* (Ann Arbor, 1980), pp. 27–31, 57–64.

14. J. H. Thiel, *A History of Roman Sea Power before the Second Punic War* (Amsterdam, 1954).

15. H. T. Wallinga, *The Boarding-Bridge of the Romans* (Groningen, 1956).

16. A. Degrassi, *Inscriptiones Latinae Liberae Rei Publicae*, 1 (Florence, 1957), no. 319. Bank Leu, *Auktion* 42 (Zürich, 1987), nos. 34 and 35, illustrates two copper bars with respectively trident and sacred chickens and suggests they were issued in connection with the Roman naval victories; the copper *as* with prow of a ship is well-known.
17. Polybius 1. 37.
18. J. H. Thiel, *Studies in the History of Roman Sea-Power in Republican Times* (Amsterdam, 1946); only G. de Sanctis, *Storia dei Romani* 3. 2 (2d ed.; Florence, 1968), p. 12, seems to comprehend the real reason why Hannibal marched by land.
19. E. S. Gruen, *The Hellenistic World and the Coming of Rome* (Berkeley, 1984), p. 271; see also A. N. Sherwin-White, *Roman Foreign Policy in the East* (London, 1984).
20. W. V. Harris, *War and Imperialism in Republican Rome 327–70 B.C.* (Oxford, 1978).
21. Appian 11. 21–22, 27, 39; A. H. McDonald and F. W. Walbank, "The Treaty of Apamea (188 B.C.): The Naval Clauses," *Journal of Roman Studies* 59 (1969), pp. 30–39.
22. According to Polybius 30. 31 Rhodian revenues sank from a million to 150,000 drachmae as a result.
23. Polybius 6. 52.
24. Meiggs, *Trees*, p. 117.
25. G. H. Tipps, "The Battle of Ecnomus," *Historia* 34 (1985), pp. 432–65, judges Roman tactics more sharply.
26. Lucretius 2. 1; E. de Saint Denis, *Le Rôle de la mer dans la poésie latine* (Paris, 1935), as corrected by Thiel, *Studies*, pp. 1–31.
27. Lycophron, *Alexandra* 1229–30; though usually dated to the early third century this particular passage seems impossible at that time and may have been interpolated. A. Momigliano, "Terra Marique," *Journal of Roman Studies* 32 (1942), pp. 53–64, takes it as referring to victory over Pyrrhus; Gruen, *Hellenistic World*, 1, p. 320, places it no earlier than success in the Second Macedonian War; S. R. West, "Lycophron Italicised?" *Journal of Hellenic Studies* 104 (1984), pp. 127–51.
28. *On the Responses of the Haruspices* 19.
29. W. Capelle, "Griechische Ethik und römischer Imperialismus," *Klio* 25 (1932), pp. 86–113; Dionysius of Halicarnassus 1. 5. 2–3; Plutarch, *de fortuna Romanorum* (*Moralia* 316C ff.).
30. P. Brulé, *La piraterie crétoise hellénistique* (Paris, 1978). We need

a newer treatment of piracy than H. A. Ormerod, *Piracy in the Ancient World* (Liverpool, 1924; reprint 1967).

31. Strabo 14. 5. 2 C668.

32. On the resurrection of Roman naval strength see the first chapter in my *Roman Imperial Navy* (2d ed.; Cambridge, 1960).

33. *On the Manilian Law* 11. 31–33; more generally on hatred of Roman injustice, *Against Verres* 3. 89.

34. Appian 12. 94–96.

35. Pliny, *Natural History* 7. 98.

36. *To Atticus* 10. 8.

37. Suetonius 16, to be preferred over Dio Cassius 48. 49. 1.

38. Appian, *Civil Wars* 5. 130.

Chapter V

1. L. Keppie, *The Making of the Roman Army* (London, 1984); J. B. Campbell, *The Emperor and the Roman Army 31 B.C.–A.D. 235* (Oxford, 1984).

2. In the following pages I have drawn on occasion from my doctoral dissertation, published as *The Roman Imperial Navy 31 B.C.–A.D. 324* (Ithaca, 1941), in a second edition by Heffer (Cambridge, 1960), and still in print by Greenwood Publishers. M. Reddé, *Mare Nostrum* (Rome, 1986), has resurveyed the subject in a very long French dissertation that does not in my judgment advance our knowledge greatly (see my review in *Gnomon*).

3. Tacitus, *Annals* 1. 9; Vegetius 4. 31 emphasizes the permanent character of the Roman navy henceforth.

4. J. H. Rose, *The Mediterranean in Ancient Times* (Cambridge, 1933), p. 120, also pp. 145–46.

5. *Roman Imperial Navy*, pp. 17–21, 23–24, with the caution that not every tombstone attests a naval station; Reddé, *Mare Nostrum*, pp. 145–319, is very full on the ports, but does not fully appreciate my warning in "Naval Activity in Greek Imperial Issues," *Revue suisse de numismatique* 46 (1967), pp. 51–57 (now in my *Essays on Ancient History*, pp. 278–84), that the presence of a naval type on a coin does not necessarily prove naval activity, especially in inland mints.

6. Ulpian, *Digest* 37. 13, "In the fleets rowers and sailors are *milites.*"

7. For C. Courtois, "Les politiques navales de l'Empire romain," *Revue historique* 186 (1939), pp. 17–47 and 225–59, and others this was the

primary reason for the creation of a permanent navy; see Reddé, *Mare nostrum,* p. 473.

8. D. Kienast, *Untersuchungen zu den Kriegsflotten der römischen Kaiserzeit* (Bonn, 1966), reviews the evidence on the status of sailors and reaches the same conclusion as that in *Roman Imperial Navy,* pp. 66–70; see also S. Panciera, *Rendiconti,* Accademia nazionale dei Lincei, classe di scienze morali, storiche e filologiche, 8. ser. 19 (1964), pp. 316–28; and the survey by Reddé, *Mare nostrum,* pp. 474–86, which is concordant.

9. *Aegyptische Urkunden aus den Koeniglichen Museum zu Berlin: Griechische Urkunden* (Berlin, 1895), no. 423, early second century from Philadelphia.

10. Mahan, *Influence of Sea Power,* p. iii; Reddé, *Mare nostrum,* p. 8, considers his primary purpose to be to illuminate the uses of the navy, but his analytical treatment (pp. 323–453) is a mixture of events over five centuries both in the Mediterranean and on the northern frontiers that is not particularly useful.

11. Apart from general treatments see K. Hopkins' survey of shipwrecks, *Journal of Roman Studies* 70 (1980), pp. 105–6 (based on A. J. Parker's statistics); J. Rougé, *Recherches sur l'organisation du commerce maritime en Méditerranée sous l'empire Romain* (Paris, 1966); J. H. D'Arms and E. C. Koepff, edd., *The Seaborne Commerce of Ancient Rome* (Rome, 1984).

12. So too even in Merovingian times pepper or papyrus warehouses existed at Massalia (Rougé, *Ships and Fleets,* p. 195).

13. Tacitus, *Annals* 3. 54, 12. 43, 15. 18; earlier 2. 59 in Augustan policy. See generally G. Rickman, *The Corn Supply of Ancient Rome* (Oxford, 1980).

14. G. Milne, *The Port of Roman London* (London, 1985); *Gallia* 30 (1972), pp. 520–22; R. Meiggs, *Roman Ostia* (Oxford, 1973); Vitruvius 5. 12 comments on the creation of artificial harbors. G. E. Rickman and G. W. Houston suggest useful questions in *American Journal of Archaeology* 90 (1986), pp. 201–2.

15. The *tabellariae* which reached port before the main fleet were sailing ships (Seneca, *Epistles* 77).

16. Strabo 3. 2. 5 C144.

17. *Digest* 4. 9. 3. 1 and 47. 9. 3 (Labeo); then 14. 2. 23 (Paulus, early third century); Hans Kreller, "Lex Rhodia," *Zeitschrift für das gesamte Handelsrecht* 85 (1921), pp. 257–367. Among praises of imperial peace on the sea see especially Epictetus 3. 13. 9.

18. See my essay "Coastal Defense in the Roman World," *American Journal of Philology* 64 (1943), pp. 56–70.

19. Arrian, *Periplus* 9.

20. Tacitus, *Histories* 1. 31.

21. E. N. Luttwak, *The Grand Strategy of the Roman Empire* (Baltimore, 1976), pp. 81ff.

22. Tacitus, *Annals* 14. 3–5; Suetonius, *Nero* 34; Dio Cassius 62. 13; L. Herrmann, "A propos du navire d'Agrippine," *Revue des études anciennes* 29 (1927), pp. 68–70.

23. Pliny, *Natural History* 9. 62; Macrobius, *Satires* 3. 16. 10. In his brief reign in 68–69 Vitellius was fabled to use the squadrons to cull luxuries for his table from Asia Minor to Spain (Suetonius, *Vitellius* 13).

24. H. Mattingly, *Coins of the Roman Empire in the British Museum,* 2 (London, 1923), p. xlvii. This issue is sometimes connected with Vespasian's victory over a Jewish fleet on an inland lake, but this seems too small an event to warrant such celebration.

25. S. Panciera, "Liburna," *Epigraphica* 18 (1956), pp. 130–56; on naval *castra* see the evidence for Gesoriacum and Dover, summed up by Reddé, *Mare nostrum*, p. 159.

26. Augustus, *Res Gestae* 26.

27. Strabo 7. 3. 13 C304 already had noted that the Romans transported their war supplies on the Danube under Augustus.

28. Dio 73. 16. 3; Scriptores Historiae Augustae, *Julianus* 6. 3–4.

29. Dio 77. 16. 7; Scriptores Historiae Augustae, *Caracalla* 5. 8; *Corpus Inscriptionum Latinorum* VI 2103a; D. van Berchem, *Museum Helveticum* 36 (1979), pp. 101–10, suggests on the basis of a naval diploma of 214 that the prefect may even so have been removed from office.

30. Zosimus 2. 22, 26 (where Licinius assembles a fleet himself by contributions from "various peoples"). Courtois, *Revue historique* 186 (1939), took this event as proof that formal naval organization had ceased to be effective; Kienast, *Untersuchungen,* disagrees, as does also Reddé, *Mare nostrum*, pp. 574ff., at great length.

31. G. Petzl and H. W. Pleket, *Zeitschrift für Papyrologie und Epigraphik* 34 (1979), p. 283, on a milestone from Lydia (A.D. 333–57).

32. E. A. Thompson, *A Roman Reformer and Inventor* (Oxford, 1952), pp. 119–20; see also M. W. C. Hassall and R. I. Ireland, *De Rebus Bellicis* (Oxford, 1979), who comment (pp. 84–89) on the use of horse-driven paddle boats from the seventeenth to the nineteenth century in both Europe and America.

33. A. Ferrill, *The Fall of the Roman Empire, The Military Explanation* (New York, 1986).
34. *Theodosian Code* 9. 40. 24, of A.D. 419.
35. Yet some kind of scratch fleets could be employed; cf. J. M. O'Flynn, *Generalissimos of the Western Roman Empire* (Edmonton, 1983), pp. 105, 110, 116.
36. Polybius 38. 21.

Epilogue

1. *Democratic Ideals and Reality* (London, 1919), p. 150.
2. Downs, *Books that Changed the World*, pp. 263ff., does follow his discussion of Mahan with an analysis of Mackinder's theory.
3. F. W. Kienitz, *Völker im Schatten* (Munich, 1981), tries to argue that Roman mastery ruined native cultural possibilities in the western Mediterranean.
4. Edward Gibbon, *Decline and Fall*, ed. J. B. Bury, 1 (London, 1909), pp. 85–86.

Bibliography

Articles, handbooks, and books of limited value are not included here.

Amit, M., *Athens and the Sea* (Brussels, 1965).

Anderson, R., *Oared Fighting Ships* (London, 1962).

Braudel, F., *The Mediterranean and the Mediterranean World in the Age of Philip II* (New York, 1973).

Brulé, P., *La piraterie crétoise hellénistique* (Paris, 1978).

Cargill, J., *The Second Athenian League* (Berkeley, 1981).

Casson, L., *The Ancient Mariners* (New York, 1959).

Casson, L., *Ships and Seamanship in the Ancient World* (Princeton, 1971).

Ericsson, C. H., *Navis Oneraria* (Åbo, 1984).

Ferrill, A., *The Fall of the Roman Empire, The Military Explanation* (New York, 1986).

Garland, R., *The Piraeus from the Fifth to the First Century B.C.* (Ithaca, 1987).

Gruen, E. S., *The Hellenistic World and the Coming of Rome* (Berkeley, 1984).

Harris, W. V., *War and Imperialism in Republican Rome, 327–70 B.C.* (Oxford, 1979).

Jordan, B., *The Athenian Navy in the Classical Period* (Berkeley, 1975).

Kienast, D., *Untersuchungen zu den Kriegsflotten der römischen Kaiserzeit* (Bonn, 1977).

Lesky, A., *Thalatta: Der Weg der Griechen zum Meer* (Vienna, 1947).

Mackinder, H., *Democratic Ideals and Reality* (London, 1919).

Mahan, A. T., *The Influence of Sea Power upon History 1660–1783* (Boston, 1890).

Meiggs, R., *The Athenian Empire* (Oxford, 1972).

Meiggs, R., *Roman Ostia* (Oxford, 1973).

Meiggs, R., *Trees and Timber in the Ancient Mediterranean World* (Oxford, 1982).

Meijer, F., *A History of Seafaring in the Classical World* (New York, 1986).

Morrison, J. S. and J. F. Coates, *The Athenian Trireme* (Cambridge, 1986).

Morrison, J. S. and R. T. Williams, *Greek Oared Ships 900–322 B.C.* (Cambridge, 1968).

Ormerod, H. A., *Piracy in the Ancient World* (Liverpool, 1924).

Reddé, M., *Mare nostrum* (Rome, 1986).

Rickman, G., *The Corn Supply of Ancient Rome* (Oxford, 1980).

Rodgers, W. L., *Greek and Roman Naval Warfare* (Annapolis, 1937).

Rougé, J., *Recherches sur l'organisation du commerce maritime en Méditerranée sous l'empire Romain* (Paris, 1966).

Rougé, J., *Ships and Fleets of the Ancient Mediterranean* (Middletown, Conn., 1981).

Saint-Denis, E. de., *Le Rôle de la mer dans la poésie latine* (Paris, 1935).

Sandars, N. K., *The Sea Peoples* (2d ed., London, 1985).

Schuller, W., *Die Herrschaft der Athener im ersten Athenische Seebund* (Berlin, 1974).

Starr, C. G., *The Roman Imperial Navy, 31 B.C.–A.D. 324* (2d ed.; Cambridge, 1960).

Starr, C. G., *Essays on Ancient History*, eds. A. Ferrill and T. Kelly (Leiden, 1979).

Tarn, W. W., *Hellenistic Military and Naval Developments* (Cambridge, 1930).

Thiel, J. H., *Studies on the History of Roman Sea Power in Republican Times* (Amsterdam, 1946).

Thiel, J. H., *A History of Roman Sea Power in Republican Times* (Amsterdam, 1954).

Thompson, E. A., *A Roman Reformer and Inventor* (Oxford, 1952).

Wallinga, W. T., The *Boarding-Bridge of the Romans* (Groningen, 1956).

Index